At the Bottom of
Shakespeare's Ocean

Shakespeare

Shakespeare Now!
Series edited by Ewan Fernie and Simon Palfrey

At the Bottom of
Shakespeare's Ocean

Steve Mentz

continuum

Continuum International Publishing Group

The Tower Building
11 York Road
London SE1 7NX

80 Maiden Lane
Suite 704
New York, NY 10038

www.continuumbooks.com

British Library Cataloguing-in-Publication Data
A catalogue record for this book is available from the British Library.

ISBN: 978-1-84706-492-9 (hardback)
       978-1-84706-493-6 (paperback)

Library of Congress Cataloging-in-Publication Data
A catalog record for this book is available from the Library of Congress.

Typeset by Newgen Imaging Systems Pvt Ltd, Chennai, India
Printed and bound in Great Britain by CPI Antony Rowe, Chippenham, Wiltshire

For Alinor, Ian, Olivia,
and the Atlantic Ocean.

Contents

Preface

Control / Stops at the shore.

(Byron)

I can tell a true story of what we feel when we face the ocean. When we float in its waves, smell its salt, hear its music, the sea commands our attention. The stories captivate us, from *The Odyssey* to "Titanic," Noah's flood to the melting polar ice. The oceans comprise the largest and least-known space on the planet, a moving body of more-than-human power and instability. We need a poetic history of the oceans, and Shakespeare, somewhat surprisingly, can help us tell one. He's not a sea-obsessed writer like Byron or Melville or Conrad, but there's more salt in his plays than you might expect. His oceans span the God-sea of the ancient world, where "they who go down to the sea in ships" see "wonders in the deep" (Psalm 107), and the boundless deeps of the early modern globe. Shakespeare's plays write the sea as opaque, inhospitable, and alluring, a dynamic reservoir of estrangement and enchantment. Full of unexpected depths and surges, it peeks out from odd corners of the plays before retreating like the tide. The first challenge of this ocean is the basic challenge the ocean always poses: to know an ungraspable thing.

We need Shakespeare's ocean now, because late-twentieth-century culture has frayed our connections to the sea. The end of the age of commercial sail and the advent of airline travel, airborne warfare, containerization, the automation of ports, and even the romance of outer space have displaced the sea from the center of our cultural imagination. Except as a place for recreation, the sea is less important to postwar Anglophone culture than to prior generations. It has become an old sailor's tale, shunted aside into maritime museums, the novels of Patrick O'Brian, and sentimental films. In geographic terms, we register this symbolic effacement in the relocation of the port of New York City – among the most important sites of economic exchange in the United States from the early Republic to the twentieth century – from downtown Manhattan across the bay to Newark, New Jersey. On the southern tip of Manhattan island, where sailors and longshoreman once walked, bankers and lawyers now stride in isolation. Nearby at the museum of South Street Seaport (formerly a thriving fish market), the 170-foot steel mainmast of the *Peking*, one of the last sailing vessels to carry commercial cargo around Cape Horn, sits dwarfed beneath the skyscrapers of Wall Street. In New York, as in major ports from Liverpool to Los Angeles, the ocean isn't the heart of the city anymore.

We don't ordinarily place the ocean at the heart of Shakespeare's plays, either. But the dramatist's engagement with the sea was neither casual nor simply metaphoric. From the opening shipwrecks of *The Comedy of Errors* (perhaps his first play) to *The Tempest* (one of his last), Shakespeare portrays the ocean as both a nearly inconceivable physical reality and a mind-twisting force for change and instability. Ariel's famous "sea-change" imagines the combined physical-and-magical powers of the ocean transfiguring human bodies. The song, like all of Shakespeare's diverse and fragmentary figurations of the ocean, isn't just a metaphor or even a description of how dramatic poetry works. It's a poet's attempt to match and figure the great waters.

To fathom Shakespeare's ocean – to go down to its bottom – requires moving in several directions at once. Each of the following chapters explores a different way that human bodies interact with the ocean: fathoming, keeping watch, swimming, beachcombing, fishing, and drowning. But the depths of Shakespeare's ocean don't emerge simply through a catalog of salty episodes. Rereading the plays from a maritime perspective connects Shakespeare to our literary culture's ongoing efforts to come to grips with the sea. Shakespeare's ocean reveals itself through contrast and continuity with the thundering seas of Romantic and post-Romantic literature, especially the vast Pacific of *Moby-Dick*, the rocky coast of Charles Olson's *Maximus Poems*, and the lyrical waters of postcolonial Caribbean poetry. Melville and Olson leave coastal New England to plunge into wild waters, and their shared monomania highlights by contrast Shakespeare's varied, musical rhythms. Caribbean poets like Édouard Glissant, Kamau Brathwaite, and Derek Walcott engage the sea as a lived-in space, its presence surrounding and informing their verse. Shakespeare's ocean, when looked at alongside these more recent writers, appears reticent. Less obsessive than Melville and more variable than Walcott, Shakespeare presents an always-moving ocean whose full meanings emerge through counterpoint with his literary heirs. Reading these authors together produces multiple visions of oceanic meaning, so that the doomed hunt for Moby-Dick speaks to Walcott's historicized sea and both reconfigure the sea-music of Shakespeare's depths.

My efforts self-consciously join what is sometimes called a "new thalassology" (from the Greek *thalassos*, the sea) that is rewriting the cultural history of the sea. Following the call to "historicize the oceans" expressed through projects like Duke University's "Oceans Connect" initiative, historians, scientists, and cultural scholars since the 1990s have been mapping the physical and cultural shapes of the oceans in world history. From the Atlantic to the Mediterranean to the Pacific, oceans have become orienting principles for the humanities and sciences. Literary scholars such as Margaret Cohen, Ian Baucom, Joseph Roach, and Bernhard Klein; historians such as Kären Wigan, Barry Cunliffe, and Marcus Rediker; and cultural theorists such as Chris Connery, Philip Steinberg, and Jean-Didier Urbain have radically expanded the cultural and historical meanings of the sea. Shakespeare's plays, written during an early phase of English maritime expansion, help us reanimate the sea's presence in Anglophone culture.

The new maritime humanities speak to at least three current critical discourses: globalization, postcolonialism, and environmentalism.

The maritime resonance of globalization emphasizes that long-distance trade and travel, historically and still today, operate largely by sea. The idea of a global space, of an ocean that spans the globe, was one of the distinctive cultural products of the early modern period. The sea's extra-territorial and multinational nature received its initiating declaration when Hugo Grotius's *Mare Liberum* (1609) served notice that the Dutch Republic would not respect the Portuguese monopoly of the East Indies trade. The "freedom of the seas" has never gone unchallenged – John Seldon's counterblast *Mare Clausum* (1635) forcefully argued for legal control of maritime routes and resources – but oceanic liberty generated a powerful cultural fantasy that Shakespeare's plays engage as a vision of poetic power.

Postcolonial perspectives recall that early modern imperialism and colonial resistance are both histories that cross oceans. Édouard Glissant's postcolonial framework of historical accumulation argues from the maritime periphery that colonization and modernization did not witness the "disenchantment" of the world, but an accumulation of empirical perspectives sedimented on top of magical thinking. The sea, as Glissant emphasizes, is both source and graveyard of history's accumulation. Glissant's theorizing extends what Derek Walcott has also suggested to the landed West: "the sea is history." In Shakespeare's England, Glissant's Martinique, and Walcott's St. Lucia, the world arrives by sea.

Finally, the sea throws cold water on the happy dreams of environmentalism. The hungry ocean destabilizes our fantasies of sustainable growth and a harmonious relationship between human culture and the natural world. Pierre Hadot's resonant articulation of two competing ideas of nature in Western culture, one Promethean – a nature humanity can control – and the other Orphic, opaque, and mysterious, provides a frame through which we can recognize the sea's environmental resonance. The ocean epitomizes Orphic nature. An oceanic perspective speaks to our emerging sense that crisis, not stability, defines the world in which we live now. Supplementing our "green" cultural turn with a "blue cultural studies" that looks at our world through the deathly, inhuman, magical lens of the sea can begin rebuilding narrative and interpretive practices to respond to our uncertain future.

Shakespeare, sitting at the heart of English literature, has more to say to these maritime discourses than we might expect. Poised on the cusp of radical changes in Western culture, Shakespeare's surging oceans prefigure the cultural floods of the scientific Enlightenment and its evil twin, Romanticist revolt. Receptive to ancient and emerging forms, Shakespeare found in the sea one of his most versatile symbols. In an early modern culture that had recently begun creating globe-shaped maps, representing the sea meant representing the world in its entirety. Shakespeare's multivalent oceans still epitomize the many ways our culture understands salt water. Hungry and musical, never-surfeited and violent, the ocean represents our alien globe. It defines the world as it is, not as we'd like it to be.

It's to the bottom of Shakespeare's ocean that this book takes you, except for one thing: we never get to the bottom. The deep sea's floor, as unreachable to early modern Europeans as the moon, is a place these plays never reach. When the sea-bed gets invoked, in Clarence's dream or Hotspur's fantasy of rescuing "drowned honor" or Prospero's mudded book, it represents the impossible fantasy of knowing the unknowable, reaching the bottom of a bottomless place. Shakespeareans know all about bottoms that "have no bottom," but the sea-floor is more than another theatrical metaphor. It was, for early modern England, a place that could not be visited but could be touched. Mariners measured the ocean's depth with a lead line (which Hotspur calls a "fathom line") that brought traces up to the surface. Andrew Marvell's *Upon Appleton House* describes the procedure:

> [A]s the mariners that sound,
> And show upon their lead the ground,
> They bring up flowers so to be seen,
> And prove they've at the bottom been.
> (381–4)

What Marvell's narrator overlooks, however, is that no one has "been" at the bottom; rather, they've brought up "flowers" from a place they never reach. Literary representations, like the lead line, reach into spaces human bodies cannot go and bring back strange things. We never reach the bottom, but we know it's there.

Acknowledgments

We're told never to swim alone, but when you're beneath the surface, there is no other way to be. Something similar is true about writing: books are at once deeply solitary and richly social products. I've been fortunate during my voyages on Shakespeare's ocean to have been buoyed by a series of wonderful institutions and guided by many salt hands. I'd like especially to thank the National Endowment for the Humanities and the Munson Institute at Mystic Seaport for their seminar in 2006. Glenn Gordinier and Eric Roorda ran a tight ship, and I'm grateful to my fellow Institute members and the many visitors who joined us in Mystic that summer. Special thanks go to Mary K. Bercaw-Edwards, who taught me to climb the rigging and set the sails on the *Charles W. Morgan,* the last whaleship left from Melville's whaling days. My maritime work has also been supported by fellowships at several great libraries, including a short-term fellowship at the Folger Shakespeare Library, a place that, like Shakespeare himself, contains more real salt than many think; a Caird Fellowship at the National Maritime Museum in London; and the R. David Parsons Fellowship at the John Carter Brown Library in Providence, Rhode Island. Ewan Fernie and Simon Palfrey have been lively and engaged series editors, and Anna Fleming and Colleen Coalter at Continuum exemplary professionals. I've traded fish stories with too many scholars, students, sailors, swimmers, and fisherfolk to list everyone by name, so I'll just say that I look forward to more voyages on literary, and literal, seas.

Chapter 1

Fathoming: *The Tempest* and *King Lear*

The ancestor speaks, it is the ocean . . . it says this race which is song, dew of song and the muffled perfume and the blue of the song, and its mouth is the song of all the mouths of foam . . .

(Édouard Glissant, "Ocean")

What does the sea in Ariel's "sea-change" mean? Readings of the song range from G. Wilson Knight's explication of tempests and music as the central metaphors of Shakespeare's career (1932) to Ian Baucom's recasting of it as the "anthem of postmodernity" (1999). For many readers, Ariel's song epitomizes the power of Shakespeare's art. It shows how poetry makes even death beautiful. This aesthetic reading has real explanatory power (plus poetic resonance, from T. S. Eliot to Sylvia Plath), but it overlooks how specifically these lines address the physical and metaphorical qualities of the ocean. The "sea-change / Into something rich and strange" (1.2.401–2) describes salt water's transformative impact on human flesh. Too often, when the song is read (or heard), the reference to the sea quickly becomes a metaphor for the artistic process or theatrical magic or mutability itself. The real taste of ocean gets lost in the flux. It shouldn't. It's there.

Poetry that contains the sea leaves a taste in the mouth, a sharp tang of nonhuman immensity. When we taste salt, we recognize instantly that this water isn't good to drink, but we also know that its bitterness flavors our world. The taste turns up in odd corners of Shakespeare's plays. Bringing these waters together enables the plays to shed light on our literature's pervasive ocean-dreams. The Francophone Caribbean poet Édouard Glissant's prose-poem "Ocean," which provides the epigraphs to this chapter, frames the sea in terms familiar from Ariel's song. Shakespeare and Glissant make odd ship-mates – the English dramatist and Caribbean poet are divided by three centuries of history, by language, and by the Atlantic Ocean – but each writer's words measure themselves against the same unfathomable depths. It's not a question of influence, exactly, though poems like "Secret Cliff," with its images of buried books and loving seas, show that Glissant knows his Shakespeare. Rather, *The Tempest* and "Ocean" both perform the same mad act of thrusting words into roiling waters. Both writers treat the sea as a challenge to poetic form. "The ancestor speaks," Glissant claims, "it is the ocean," and in this poem the sea-change that transfigures death refigures history. For both writers, the poet's voice blends with the voice of the surf, "and its mouth is the song of all the mouths of foam."

It's understandable that readers don't always think Ariel's song is really about the sea, since the idea that the sea needs singing – as opposed to just seeing – can seem strange. When we stand at its edge, the sea appears at once too vast and too obvious for inquiry. In the modern West, the ocean is everywhere and nowhere, at once the most meaningful and most overlooked feature of our cultural imagination. The sea is a physical object of almost inconceivable weight – the largest thing on the planet – and a vessel of inchoate symbolic meanings. The white noise of the surf represents the ultimate blank, a song beyond history and perhaps beyond meaning itself. For modern thinkers from Freud to Fellini, the ocean shadows the unconscious, a vast subterranean place of unexpressed meaning and fecundity. For much of modern culture, the sea cannot be represented; it is too large for history, too vast for culture, too fluid for any stable meaning.

Plunging into Shakespeare's ocean can help replace this amorphous, distant sea with a more exact sense of the ocean's presence in our literary and cultural histories. The sea's full salty immensity is seldom or never present in the plays – death by drowning is always a threat, rarely a fact – but when the ocean appears, even in metaphor, it wrenches us out of our land-based perspectives. The water-world is not exactly foreign; it directly influences our physical bodies and cultural history. The sea's shocking and uncomfortable touch, the plays suggest, typifies our relationship with an untrustworthy natural environment. This unstable place increasingly resembles our world today.

The sea has always been around us, to borrow Rachel Carson's phrase, and the story of how human meaning attaches to the oceans comprises a full history of Western culture. In Shakespeare's era familiar representations of the sea encountered new realities. To the ancient world the sea was the terrifying face of an angry God, as it appeared to Noah and Odysseus and Jonah. In the Anglo-Saxon lyric poem "The Seafarer," the rime-cold sea represents exile and misery, but its immensity also "yells and incites me onto the whale's road." The sea's treacherous lure would later attract Romantic poets like Byron and Coleridge, for whom the deep blue provided vistas for individual transformation. In the early modern period, however, as sailors pioneered sea-routes around the horns of Africa and South America and across the Atlantic and Pacific basins, the oceans became highways of European expansion. Classical and biblical precedents cautioned that the sea should be shunned. Plato argues that the ideal city should be built no less than eleven miles away from the shore (*Laws* 4), and the Book of Revelation looks forward to a time when "there would be no more sea" (21). Even biblical verses that emphasize travail on the waters, including Psalm 107's claim that seafarers discover "the works of the Lord," contrast foolhardy sailors with sensible landlubbers who stay dry. (In this, the Psalm and "The Seafarer" agree.) The transoceanic turn of early modern European culture reshaped the cultural meanings of the ocean, so that it became not just hostile or divine, but also a space for human activity, risk, and opportunity.

The boundless deep teemed with competing symbolic charges in early modern culture, as interpreters of God's judgment contested the careful plotting of compass variation and both discourses played off the efforts of merchants, conquerors, and colonizers to derive value from the oceans. In these exchanges, the sea's mysteries became urgent; the ocean needed to be understood even as it frustrated understanding. We can hear sea-fever building in early modern works of hydrography and navigation. Robert Norman's *Safeguard of Sailors*, his 1584 translation of the Dutch "great Rutter," advances multiple reasons "to prefer Hydropgraphie or Nauigation before any other art and science." The first reason is economic: maritime activities support "the whole bodie of the common welth," rather than just some of the nation's competing parts. In his second reason, however, Norman hits upon the metaphor Joseph Conrad would use for his memoir: the sea is culture's mirror. You can see in the waters, Norman claims "(as it were in a mirror) . . . the inestimable bounty and infinite goodness of the Lord." The sentiment echoes Psalm 107 as well as Conrad's *The Mirror of the Sea*, but Norman applauds not so much God's mysteries as the emerging sciences of hydrography and navigation, which make the sea legible. God has, Norman emphasizes, "from aboue infused this so excellent a skill [i.e., navigation] into the mindes of men." When Isaac Vossius, one of Europe's first real ocean scientists, expands Norman's claims in *Treatise Concerning the Motion of the Seas and Winds* (1677, Latin ed. 1663), he insists that the sea is a mystery ("this fluid Element seems to baffle and scorn the measure of human understanding") and also that he can discern in the ocean the "noble and constant order of nature, which suffers nothing to happen by chance or fortune." The early modern sea, like Glissant's Caribbean and Melville's "mysterious, divine" Pacific, baffles as it entices. No longer distant or entirely supernatural, it becomes instead the salt tang of the world as it truly exists.

This sea-change in early modern oceanic meaning from divine mystery to primal reality reminds us that even the trackless sea has a history. We recognize Shakespeare's ocean, but its meanings are not exactly ours. Between us roll the vast depths of Romanticism. For Byron, perhaps the most famous swimmer of the nineteenth century, the "deep and dark blue Ocean" represents the true face of Nature, the thing that always exceeds humanity's control. "Time writes no wrinkle on thine azure brow," he sings, "Such as creation's dawn beheld, thou rollest now." Herman Melville, perhaps the most intense extrapolator of Shakespeare's sea-poetry, echoes Byron on the last page of *Moby-Dick*: "the great shroud of the sea rolled on as it rolled five thousand years ago." (Victor Hugo's sea-epic, *Toilers of the Sea*, also sounds the same concluding note: "There was now nothing but the sea.") But Melville, like Shakespeare, did not only use the sea as symbol of eternity. Both writers' figurations of the sea mix the transcendent and the tangible. Shakespeare's sea, like Walcott's, is history, but it is also poetry (like Glissant's), eternity (like Byron's), and many other things besides (like Melville's). Shakespeare's ocean bears its meaning both inside and athwart history. Current efforts (including my own) to historicize the ocean carry some risks: to historicize is to set boundaries, and the sea always overspills its borders. The infinite sea, however, is ending today in a very literal sense, as marine ecologists and commercial fishermen encounter the sea's physical limits. Shakespeare's sea, which predates Byron's, can correct the lingering glow of Romanticist plenitude. The early modern sea speaks to us across the Romantic gap.

If the sea is around us, it is also always outside us; it is the place on earth that remains inimical to human life. Even though our bodies, like our planet, are more than two-thirds water, we can't live in the sea. The most fundamental physical feature of the ocean, for poets, scientists, fishermen, and swimmers alike, is neither its mutable form nor its vastness, but its inhospitality: it's the place in the world where human bodies, if they are there too long, die. To be more precise, water is the place where we used to live – in evolutionary and biological terms – but can't any more. Shakespeare captures this estrangement by figuring the ocean as a terrifyingly lost paradise, an Eden so unattainable that we can't imagine it as home anymore. This place may be "rich," but it is also "strange." We can't go there to stay. The Romantic (Byronic) sense that the sea represents the ultimate truth of Nature resists this alienation and insists that the sea is what we most desire. Shakespeare, by contrast, recognizes the pull of the sea but doesn't sentimentalize it. Like Melville, Shakespeare finds in the ocean reflections of both world and self. In Ishmael's formulation, humanity sees its own face in the waters, transfigured into "the image of the ungraspable phantom of life." Shakespeare's plays, written during a key phase of Western culture's oceanic turn, contain a series of attempts to grasp this phantom.

Shakespeare approached the ocean as a poet and professional dramatist. It's likely that he saw the sea, perhaps swam in it or sailed on it, but unlikely that he voyaged extensively across it. For the playwright, the sea serves as theatrical device as well as salty reality, and the needs of individual plays shape his attempts to represent maritime meaning. But Shakespeare's representations of the ocean taken as a whole, from Ariel's "never-surfeited sea" (3.3.55) to the "enchaféd flood" that drowns the Turkish fleet in *Othello*, comprise fragments of a poetic portrait, comparable in insight if not intensity to *Moby-Dick*. Shakespeare's career-long engagement with the sea reveals a deep meditation on the ocean as unattainable physical object and variable symbolic topos. I begin by following Ariel's song to the bottom of Shakespeare's ocean, where it reveals among corpses, pearls, and coral a vision of theatrical change and human alienation.

The Sea That Changes

> . . . *ocean! You permit, you are accomplice, maker of stars; how is it you do not open your wings into a voracious lung? . . .*
>
> (*Édouard Glissant, "Ocean"*)

So, with an ear for the sea, let's listen again to Ariel's familiar words –

Full fathom five thy father lies,
Of his bones are coral made;
Those are pearls that were his eyes,

Nothing of him that doth fade
But doth suffer a sea-change
Into something rich and strange.
    Sea nymphs hourly ring his knell . . .
    Ding dong . . . ding dong bell.
                    (1.2.397–403, 405)

There's more real salt here than we notice at first. The variable three- and four-beat rhythm recalls the ocean's audible presence, its constant, repetitive, "hourly" music. "Coral" and "pearls" are maritime treasures that populate the inaccessible depths with things we can see and touch. On a basic level the song's narrative – the sea-change itself – hardens oceanic fluidity into artistic reality. The song insists that we see not the ocean but the things the sea has changed. It's a story about death and encroaching stillness, from the breathless alliterative opening to the two closing couplets. Its poetic meaning embraces the dissolving chemistry of the sea, a process W. H. Auden describes, in *The Sea and the Mirror,* his poetic meditation on *The Tempest,* as "the silent dissolution of the sea / Which misuses nothing because it values nothing." Submerging a human body in salt water creates beauty, and death.

Long treated a keystone of Shakespeare's artistry and invoked by modern poets both canonical (T. S. Eliot's "The Waste Land") and postcolonial (Kamau Brathwaite's jazz-inflected "full flatten- / ed fifth"), Ariel's song serves two functions in *The Tempest,* one narrative and the other metaphorical. In narrative terms, it facilitates the play's recovery from the opening disaster, using a vision of undersea treasure to draw Ferdinand away from his past (Alonso) toward his future (Miranda). In symbolic terms, the song represents the transforming powers of oceanic magic. But we too seldom remember that this musical ocean is false. All the stories the song tells are lies: there is no dead King beneath the waters, and Ariel's music, which works "I'th' air, or th' earth" (1.2.388), salvages neither coral nor pearls. The real ocean creates change, but not through happy fictions. *The Tempest,* like *Moby-Dick,* tells a story of radical transformation wrought by exposure to the sea. Melville's tragic intensity seems an odd match for Shakespeare's lyricism, but both works present broken voyages – Prospero and Miranda's expulsion from Milan, Alonso's return from Algiers, Ahab's search for the white whale – that complicate the utopian simplicity of Ariel's vision. We never find the treasures the song promises. The sea-change instead captures the force, physical and metaphoric, of salt water transfiguring flesh. There is something terrifying about Ariel's description of radical physical metamorphosis, and its insistence on a glittering but false vision of submerged treasure. Taking the measure of these waters is nearly impossible and also irresistible.

Reading for the salt means casting off familiar ties, so my explication of Ariel's song focuses less on famous phrases like "sea-change" or "rich and strange" than on the maritime term "fathom." This word hides itself inside the ostentatiously musical opening line: "Full fathom five . . . father." A rich, old Anglo-Saxon word, fathom derives its meaning from the width of two arms stretched out (OED 1) and had come by Shakespeare's time to be a common measure of underwater distance and depth. (A standard fathom is six feet.) This maritime word orders and measures the ocean. Sea terms, as readers of Patrick O'Brian novels know, resonate with land-bound readers because they capture the intense alterity of life at sea. Landlubbers don't understand the vocabulary, but we recognize what happens when labor works. Technical maritime terminology has generated hosts of now-dead metaphors, from "the bitter end" (which refers to the inboard end of an anchor cable) to "by and large" (which means sailing both into and with the wind). The appropriation of sea terms registers landed culture's fascination with the difficulty of living in close contact with the ocean. The word fathom spins its technical meaning into a richly applicable metaphor: to fathom means either to find a depth, as with a sounding line, or to discern a hidden meaning (OED 4b).

Five fathoms, thirty feet, separate Ferdinand from the treasures his father's body has (supposedly) become. The distance seems oddly short. At thirty feet, the King's body straddles the boundary between the accessible and inaccessible sea. This depth of water, one strong swimmer's breath away from the surface, is all that separates Ferdinand from his father's glittering corpse. The magical place is under water, but not really out of reach. Ferdinand, a strong swimmer (see 2.1.115–22) who will later be imagined in his father's place, "mudded in that oozy bed" (5.1.151), could have swum to the coral were he not entranced by Ariel's music. The song presents a sea-floor we can almost visit, an ocean at the margins of human comprehension. By singing so lucidly to Ferdinand of a place that neither visits, Ariel infects the prince with his own waywardness and filial impiety. Ferdinand does not swim to his father because the waters intervene, and also because the sea-song has begun to change him, making him less fixed in his own self. He can see but not quite make sense of the sea. Even the song's compact six-line "Venus and Adonis" stanza (ababcc) gets distorted when the sea nymphs displace Ariel's voice with an awkward, partly legible final couplet ("knell . . . ding-dong bell"). The nymphs, divine figures of the metamorphic sea, disrupt poetic closure, and then recreate it.

Ariel's music imposes poetic structure on human mortality, and also, in its lyric fluidity, the song suggests that, to match the sea, humans and poetic forms must open themselves to disorder. Now that the King is (imaginatively) gone, everything he represents – political order, social hierarchy, human plans – gets transfigured in the deathly fertility of the ooze. A new marine logic replaces the land-bound world. The long exposition that fills the next scene (1.2) shows how thoroughly the sea undergirds the play's central narratives. All this scene's stories are sea stories. First, Prospero educates Miranda about the "sea-storm" (1.2.177). Next he supplies the sentimental back-story of their exile, which he terms their "sea-sorrow" (1.2.170). Finally Ariel sings about the "sea-change." Sea-sorrow, sea-storm, sea-change: the three compounds trace the play's past, present, and future plots. The political crisis of Prospero's dukedom creates sorrow, the storm brings disorder to the island, and then everything gets reconfigured through magical change. The sea writes all the play's plots.

The three compounds invoke three different seas. The chaotic "storm" imagines a hostile ocean, familiar from the Book of Jonah, "The Seafarer," and *Moby-Dick*. Prospero's history of "sorrow," by contrast, imagines the castaways as passive victims of an opaque but finally sympathetic power. The contrast seems instructive: those who struggle against the sea, like the sailors on the Neapolitan flagship, get wrecked (or nearly so), but those who submit to it, like Prospero and Miranda, get rescued. (It's on this second, magical sea that the nautical saints of medieval legends sail, from *The Golden Legend*'s Mary Magdalene to Cunstance in "The Man of Law's Tale.") The final term, "change," constructs the sea as a poetic and narrative opportunity; this is Shakespeare's sea of stories and also Glissant's "accomplice, [and] maker of stars." Shakespeare's play employs all three forms: the redemptive sorrow-flashback, the near-tragic storm, and utopian futures driven by "change."

To reach Ariel's false bottom requires that we acquiesce to the guidance of nonhuman spirits and that we value beauty more than life. His cruel aesthetic rejects land-bound stability. First roiling and then calming the waters creates space for Prospero's revenge and marriage plots. But the play's island-stories never quite recapture the opening scene's taste of salt. As the Neapolitan ship appears to be sinking, Gonzalo describes a nightmare sea, with "every drop of water . . . gap[ing] at widest to glut" (1.1.58–9). Ariel's song and Prospero's magic never quite redeem this open-mouthed ocean. Rather, the song measures the five-fathom distance between life and death, and then provides the fortunate prince with a young maiden as his life raft. He might have dove for the bottom, but chose not to.

Sailing Away

> . . . *And see! there remains only the sum of the song and the eternity of voice and childhood already of those who will inherit it. Because as far*

> *as suffering is concerned it belongs to all: everyone has its vigorous*
> *sand between their teeth . . .*
>
> (Édouard Glissant, "Ocean")

Ariel's song is not the only part of *The Tempest* in which we often overlook the sea. Just as the song encourages readings that focus on artistry and poetic power – readings my fathom-fueled plunge into maritime particularity have sought to complicate – so the play's opening scene calls up a political context in which the Boatswain's cry, "What cares these roarers for the name of king?" (1.1.16–17), suggests that Shakespeare anticipates our democratic disdain for monarchs. There is real political force in this cry and this scene, in which regal "authority" cannot control the wild waves. The raging ocean fuels a chaotic resistance to monarchism. But often antiauthoritarian readings of this scene show the same partial blindness as aesthetic readings of "Full fathom five": they make sense of Shakespeare by ignoring the sea. Politics plays a major role in the storm scene – the King, his brother, his son, his ally (Antonio), and his counselor (Gonzalo) elbow their way into the crowd of working sailors (1.1.8), and later three of these men return (1.1.36) – but the heart of the scene stages dangerous maritime work trying to preserve a threatened community. The storm insists, in Glissant's phrase, that "as far as suffering is concerned it belongs to us all." *The Tempest* begins with an encounter between human labor, technical language, and the ungovernable sea. The Boatswain's work attempts the same task as Ariel's magic, but what Ariel calms the Boatswain cannot master.

If "fathom" defines Ariel's maritime vocabulary, the Boatswain's key technical term is "yare" or "yarely." The Boatswain and Master repeat the word four times (1.1.3, 1.1.6 twice, and 1.1.33), using it as an intensifying adverb ("fall to't yarely"), a command to work quickly ("Yare! Yare!"), and perhaps an expletive ("Yare! . . . A plague on this howling"). Another old Anglo-Saxon word kept in use by seamen, yare means quickly or thoroughly (OED 1 and 2). It captures the hurried but exact labor of sailors in a crisis. To work yarely means matching the water's swiftness with human labor, and if "yare" lacks the full metaphoric force of "fathom," that may be because this kind of work is too fast (and too technical) for clear symbolic resonance. We like our shipboard work to be yare, but we can't always interpret it as it's happening. The two scenes' sea terms epitomize different aspects of Shakespeare's ocean: to fathom (1.2) means dive to the bottom, as Ariel's song figures the sea-bed as a space between art and death, and yare (1.1) means to work as quickly and completely as possible, as the sailors grapple with the physical reality of the sea. The Boatswain's effort to "Fall to't yarely" (1.1.3) define human labor's attempts to engage the sea. It preserves the ship, but Ariel's magic – his "flam'd amazement" and "sight-outrunning" fires (1.2.198, 204) – still controls the play.

The Boatswain's maritime language has created controversy among nautical readers, at least one of whom, A. F. Falconer, thinks that Shakespeare renders seamanship so accurately that he must have gone to sea during the "lost years" of 1584–90. Even though this claim seems unwarranted, the Boatswain's technical language functions as a prose prebuttal to Ariel's lyricism. Ariel's nonhuman speed and power represents the sea's supernatural terror. Against the spirit's flames and divisions, the mariners rely on skilled labor. Their general task seems clear enough; they steer the ship away from a dangerous shoreline. On the open sea, land represents danger, and the first appeal to supernatural powers in this magically dense play is the Boatswain's address to the storm: "Blow til thou burst thy wind, if room enough" (1.1.7–8). Asking for sea-room in a phrase that recalls a mariner's plea in *Pericles* ("Blow, and split thyself," 3.1.44) and Lear's cry to the storm ("Blow winds and crack your cheeks!" 3.2.1), the Boatswain emphasizes that a landless sea is a safe sea. All of his commands seek to maximize the room around the ship. He asks the men to "Take in the topsail" (1.1.6) to decrease their forward speed. When that fails he removes the topmast entirely (1.1.33). Then he "bring[s] her to try with the main course" (1.1.34) – the "main course" is the lowest sail on the mainmast and bringing "to try" means sailing into the wind and steering off the lee shore. This tactic fails as well, so the Boatswain resorts to the hardest-to-understand sea term in Shakespeare's plays, "Lay her a-hold, a-hold! Set her two courses off to sea again!" (1.1.48–9). No early modern sea manuals show the term "a-hold," but the effort seems to be to set the two main sails ("courses") to gain forward momentum and escape the island. The word a-hold may be Shakespeare's or a printer's error for "a-hull," which means lie under no sail and hope to ride out the storm, but that maneuver does not involve any courses. Perhaps Shakespeare, a landlubber after all, could not resist the metaphoric ring of "a-hold," which captures the Boatswain's attempt to protect his ship through expert labor and technical language.

Neither words nor seamanship can hold back the sea, and the scene ends with a "confused noise within" (1.1.60SD) and apparent chaos. It violates all rules of dramatic structure to introduce characters only to drown them immediately, and few audiences have been surprised that Gonzalo's plea for a safe landfall gets answered. But this scene's vision of watery death ("We split, we split" [1.1.60], cry the mariners) never really goes away. It is this sea that Ariel's music covers up when he rhymes "kissed" with "wild waves whist" (1.2.378–9). After 1.2 we trust Prospero that the storm has passed with "no harm" (1.2.15). We similarly rely on his later assurance that he can provide "calm seas, [and] auspicious gales" (5.1.315) for the journey home, although he has drowned his magic book. Here and elsewhere his magical displays, including his masque, attempt to control the sea or leave it behind, rather than engaging its metamorphic power. The Boatswain's last line in the first scene, however, registers the bodily limits of any human encounter with the sea: "What," he laments, "must our mouths be cold?" (1.1.51). Prospero's magical show-and-tell never really faces this question. The cold mouth of a (supposedly) doomed sailor inverts the pearl eyes of the (supposedly) dead king: this is what happens to human bodies underwater. It's a terrifying prospect from which *The Tempest* recoils. Death by drowning: even this play can't really show it.

Fathom and Half: *King Lear*

> *. . . The ocean is patience, its wisdom is the tare of time.*
> (*Édouard Glissant, "Ocean"*)

The Tempest escapes the waters through music and magic, but a salt taste lingers. Perhaps the starkest intrusion of the ungraspable ocean in Shakespeare's plays comes, however, in a series of land-bound scenes. The storm scenes of *King Lear* transform the land Cordelia calls "our sustaining corn" (4.4.6) into a nightmare seascape. These scenes preemptively invert Ariel's redemptive song. With our ears attuned to Shakespeare's ocean, we hear in the storm scenes (3.1–2, 4, 6) what we saw in New Orleans in 2005: the hungry ocean gaining advantage on the kingdom of the shore (Sonnet 64). Lear's suffering anticipates Ariel's story but narrates it from the point of view of the drowned king. One of Lear's knights describes the storm as an anti-sea-change when he reports that the king, "Bids the wind blow the earth into the sea, / Or swell the curled waters 'bove the main, / That things might change, or cease" (3.1.5–7). Lear demands what Ariel's song deceptively offers Ferdinand, change and death. Gloucester, faced with chaos, longs for a Prospero to control the sea: "The sea, with such a storm as his bare head / In hell-black night endured, would have buoyed up / And quenched the stelled fires" (3.7.58–60). Imagining a catastrophic version of a proto-ecological system in which the sea's water quenches the lightning's fire, Gloucester recalls Miranda, who also hopes for fire and water to cancel each other out: "The sky, it seems, would pour down stinking pitch / But that the sea, mounting to the welkin's check, / Dashes the fire out" (1.2.3–5). Both characters imagine oceans as parts of stable systems, with an internal balance that prevents either too much fire or too much water. In *The Tempest*, Prospero and Ariel provide that order. In *King Lear*, no one can.

The most resonant observations of oceanic chaos come from Edgar, who measures rising waters within the hovel with the word that would later become Ariel's maritime touchstone. When Lear is about to follow the Fool inside, Edgar's off-stage voice interrupts: "Fathom and half: fathom and half! Poor Tom!" (3.4.37; F only). As he describes (or imagines) the hovel, it's full of water, nine feet deep (a fathom and a half), already over his head. Water has filled up this last human refuge, making it as inhospitable as the world outside. Edgar sees, more clearly than the other characters, that this play has no safe or sustainable shelter. The image of the Bedlam beggar floating inside the hovel forecloses any hoped-for political or familial reconciliation. Lear has tried to salvage a moral order in his just-expressed desire to "Take physic, pomp . . . And show the heavens more just" (3.4.33–6). But while the king can imagine caring for the "poor naked wretches" (3.4.28), his regenerative vision crashes head-long into Edgar's watery madness. No king can control the sea.

After this scene, Edgar's waters spill onto the rest of the play, so that in its second half *King Lear* becomes, strangely, a maritime play. More precisely, in its insistence on looking at human suffering as nakedly as possible, the play paints a maritime picture. To explain the contrast between an inhospitable world and his more disorderly mind, Lear contrasts land-bound dangers with oceanic ones: "Thou'dst shun a bear, / But if thy flight lay toward the roaring sea, / Thou'dst meet the bear i'the mouth" (3.4.9–11). Previewing the choice between bear and stormy sea of *The Winter's Tale* (3.3), Lear's agony brings him, and his play, to the water's edge. When he tears at his clothes ("Off, off, you lendings," 3.4.106), the Fool warns him not about nakedness but immersion: "Prithee, nuncle, be contented; 'tis a naughty night to swim in" (3.4.108–9). The kingdom has become a sea and its buildings a fathom and half flood: in this world, Lear should learn to swim.

In the play's remaining acts, other characters see the kingdom's disorder in maritime terms. Albany, who especially in the Q text serves as a moral chorus, explains the play's oceanic turn: "It will come: / Humanity must perforce play on itself, / Like monsters of the deep" (4.3.49–51, Q only). His vision of waters leads to cannibalism and a proto-Hobbesian war of all against all. Cordelia, too, connects her father's madness to the taste of salt: "Why, he was met even now / As mad as the vexed sea, singing aloud . . ." (4.4.1–2). The disorder that Albany finds in the world-made-sea Cordelia locates in her father's mind. For both characters the sea represents a world out of control. All systems of moral and political order have broken down. The predatory ocean floods the sustaining corn.

In the sea-world of these final acts, Edgar's radical theatricalism provides a last desperate survival tactic. When he tempts his blind father toward the false Dover cliffs, Edgar invokes the ocean as the principle of reality, even though there isn't really any water there. "Hark, do you hear the sea?" (4.6.4), he calls to his father on the bare stage. When Gloucester completes his verse line by saying "No, truly" (4.6.4), on one level he simply indicates that even the blind don't easily mistake Edgar's theatrical conceits for reality. On another level, however, this exchange emphasizes that Edgar's play-acting, like his "fathom and half" warning, attempts to engage maritime disorder from a human perspective.

Edgar's description of Dover Beach, far below the imaginary verge to which he tempts his father, gives the ocean provisional order. Acting pits itself against the sea, and momentarily the waters shrink and seem less terrifying:

> The fishermen that walk on the beach
> Appear like mice, and yon tall anchoring barque
> Diminished to her cock, her cock a buoy
> Almost too small for sight. The murmuring surge
> That on th'unnumbered idle pebble chafes,
> Cannot be heard so high. I'll look no more,
> Lest my brain turn and the deficient sight
> Topple down headlong.

> (4.6.17–24)

The passage's double movement captures Edgar's attempt to theatricalize the sea. He does not humanize the waters so much as internalize their disorder. His imaginary kingdom, still at "fathom and half" depth, opens itself to oceanic chaos and change. In this world, big things get smaller: men are mice, barques cock-boats, and cock-boats buoys. The "murmuring surge" provides a hint of sea-music (like Ariel's song) but doesn't threaten the "idle pebble." The ocean isn't hungry but peaceful. This sea, however, is both fictional and distant; its song "cannot be heard so high," and the image taken whole – the sea and the cliff – disorients Edgar. His fear of falling is a fear of madness ("Lest my brain turn") and looking over the imaginary verge draws him back into the horror of the sea. Edgar's play-acting aims, as he later says, to "cure" his father, and to do so he replaces the fearful ocean with a gentle surge. The theatrical gambit creates mixed results: Gloucester eschews suicide, but Edgar's revealed identity later bursts his heart. Edgar's final encounter with his brother, in which he transforms himself into the masked knight of chivalry, drags the play back to the land. Dramatic mobility assures his personal survival, but at considerable cost.

Edgar's theatrical restlessness, what we might call his ocean within, generates a pattern in the second half of *King Lear* that I'll call the false-floor effect. Whenever it seems as if the play has bottomed out, whenever a floor beneath the suffering seems to have been reached, a new catastrophe opens to plunge us further into the depths. "Fathom and half": the play repeatedly falls into the depths. I count four false floors in the second half of *King Lear*. The first time this pattern appears, when Edgar's "fathom and half" flood undermines Lear's desire for political reform, the floor opens with specifically maritime imagery. Later, after Edgar's imaginary Dover beach makes the waters momentarily palatable, the new moral baseline he creates – "Bear free and patient thoughts" (4.6.80), he advises his father – falls headlong into the shock of reality, in this case through the stage direction, "Enter Lear, mad." (The word "mad" appears in Q only, and many editions add some variation of Capell's eighteenth-century interpolation, "fantastically dressed with wild flowers.") The king's broken mind undermines Edgar's plea for patience the same way Gloucester's ruined eyes previously frustrate his earlier attempt to philosophize after the storm. Then, Edgar consoles himself that he is better off having faced the storm's harshness: "Yet better thus, and known to be contemned / Than still contemned and flattered" (4.1.1–2). His blind father's entrance, however, pulls the rug out from beneath his stoic acceptance of human misery: "Who is't can say 'I am at the worst'? . . . / the worst is not / So long as we can say, 'This is the worst.'" (4.1.27, 29–30). These false floors reach a climax with the entrance of Lear in the final scene, "with Cordelia in his arms" (5.3.254SD). In three of these four examples, the fall emerges from silent stage action, not dialogue: language falters before the entrances of Gloucester (blind), Lear (mad), and Cordelia (dead). Edgar's "fathom and half" warning initiates a pattern in which extra-linguistic actions disrupt language's attempts to create order. His open theatricality defers a reckoning with the sea, blindness, madness, and death, but by accepting and internalizing them, not constructing a stable place outside them.

King Lear's death-soaked seascape mirrors and preemptively undermines *The Tempest*'s poetic transformations. In both plays the sea represents a basic inhuman-ness, an alterity that defines Shakespeare's ocean throughout his career. Read as phases in a continued poetic investigation, these portraits of ocean (like Glissant's) present limit cases. Human bodies plunge into hostile seas, and poetic forms attempt their salvage. From his earliest to his last plays, Shakespeare's sea-poetry presents a bitter ecology of salt. Ariel's theatrical magic and Lear's anguished loss share the common insight that the sea is not our home. But the intimate knowledge that immersion produces in characters from Egeon in *The Comedy of Errors* to Trinculo in *The Tempest* also suggests that the ocean generates strange and powerful knowledge. Glissant, writing from the warm waters of Martinique, emphasizes the ocean's "patience" and "wisdom." At the bottom of Shakespeare's ocean we glimpse treasure and death, but we can't bring these things to the surface. What we end up looking at, instead, is the water itself.

Chapter 2
Keeping Watch: *Othello*

The sea was born of the earth without the sweet union of love . . .
(*Charles Olson*, The Maximus Poems)

It's sea water that mads Othello. Salt is what he can't understand.
Surrounded by ocean on the venereal island of Cyprus, delivered
from the sea-storm that sinks the Turks, caught between his newly
traveled wife and the ancient who is saltier than he appears, Othello
cannot accommodate changing seas. His desperate longing for calm
after tempest, port after storm, represents an attempt to pass through
oceanic disorder into a calm world. While some tragic heroes
(especially Hamlet and Antony) learn from the mind-stretching sea,
Othello craves stability and dry land. He has navigated the seas, and
he knows the value of maritime treasures, including a daughter of
the Venetian sea-empire, but his poetic language, including his final
reference to his "journey's end . . . [the] butt / And very sea-mark of
[his] utmost sail" (5.2.265–6), tries to limit the waters and mark the
unmarkable. It's no surprise that these tactics do not work. In his
play, as in our world, little islands lie encircled by Ocean.

Shipwreck with Spectators

The sea
is right up against the skin of the shore with a tide
as high
as this one . . .
("*December 22nd*," The Maximus Poems)

The sea surrounds this play, but we don't see it much. It's hard to pin down. The play stages human efforts to keep watch over the ocean in 2.1, in which a crowd of shore-bound characters stand in the position of Miranda in *The Tempest*, gathered on the coast of Cyprus to watch the aftermath of a great storm. Having moved from canal-riddled Venice to Cytherea's island, the play foregrounds its fascination with and inability to understand the ocean. "What from the cape can you discern at sea?" asks governor Montano, to which a gentleman replies "Nothing at all" (2.1.1–2). Like Othello's watch over his wife's chastity, the Venetian watch on the sea frustrates itself because it cannot gain certain knowledge. The waters (and the wife) baffle interpretation. "[I]t is a high-wrought flood," continues the Gentlemen, "I cannot 'twixt the haven and the main / Descry a sail" (2.1.3–4). Two significant fixtures of maritime description operate here. First, the seascape contains opposites. The split between landed "haven" and watery "main" reinscribes the border between land and sea. This border, here as in many other classical and early modern passages, also figures the division between heaven and hell. (The Q text reads "heaven" for "haven"; this textual indeterminacy underlines the small representational gap between human havens and supernatural heavens.) Second, the sea reveals a basic truth about high-wrought waters: they make it hard to see. The "desperate tempest" (2.1.21) frustrates human interpretive abilities. The gentlemen know what the storm does – it wrecks the Turkish fleet, spares the Venetians, and provides an emblem of celestial "designment" (2.1.22) – but they see "nothing at all." In language that parallels Iago's insistent negation, the second gentleman understands the storm's symbolic power but not what it is:

> The chidden billow seems to pelt the clouds,
> The wind-shaked surge, with high and monstrous mane,
> Seems to cast water on the burning bear
> And quench the guards of th'ever-fired pole.

I never did the like molestation view
On the enchafed flood.

$$(2.1.12–17)$$

He makes sense of the storm by not-seeing it, through "seems" and "quench[ings]" and things "never . . . view[ed]." Unlike Miranda, who has Prospero to lecture her after the storm, no one supplements these gentlemen's interpretations with substantial knowledge.

Watching a storm from the safety of land provides a privileged point of view from which insight is possible. For the Roman poet Lucretius, the shipwreck with spectator paradigm creates philosophy. "It is pleasant," Lucretius writes, "when the winds stir up the waters on the great sea, to see [*spectare*] another man's troubles [*laborem*]" (*De rerum natura*, 2.1–2). This humanist topos, quoted by Montaigne and Robert Burton, among others, emphasizes the power of the philosophical mind, resting firm on the bedrock of reason, to make sense of the world's disorder. In *The Tempest*, Shakespeare mines this framework for its pedagogic structure, and Prospero turns the spectacle into a history lesson that puts his student to sleep. The lesson in *Othello* isn't quite so neat. On a political level, the storm solves Venice's problems; "our wars are done," says the third gentleman (2.1.20). But Lucretius's paradigm insists that shipwreck has philosophical implications. Othello cannot be a successful philosopher, however, because he is not a spectator; instead, he himself is "lost . . . on a dangerous sea" (2.1.46). In a scene full of classical parallels – the heaven/hell span of the waves echoes a descriptive topos that Shakespeare may have known from Ovid, Virgil, Lucan, Psalm 107, and the Book of Jonah, among other places – the "shipwreck with spectator" motif insists that the storm generates philosophical insight. It's typical of, even essential to, this play that physical opacity should produce (or almost produce) philosophical meaning. In *Othello*, "not" generates meaning. This deep nihilism, voiced primarily but not exclusively by Iago, insists that we peer into the storm's disorder not to see with metaphysical clarity but to face our own inability to see.

The sense that looking at the sea invites and frustrates human attempts to philosophize their conditions connects *Othello* to Charles Olson's *Maximus Poems* (1960–75). Olson's massive collection of lyrics, prose poems, and short narratives combines personal episodes, Greek myth, aesthetic speculation, and the early modern and modern maritime history of Gloucester, Massachusetts. Sea and self lie entangled at the center of his verse. For Olson-as-Maximus, the high tide that stretches "right up against the skin of the shore" disfigures any purely earth-bound meanings. Olson's postmodern epic, like *Othello*, recognizes that the sea is an essential element in human life precisely because it disrupts interpretation. The waters are born of the earth, Olson recalls via Hesiod, but "without the sweet union of love." The poet-narrator Maximus, unlike Othello, never tries to replace a sea-story with a love-story. His poems instead show the sea infiltrating a human imagination, seeping into its corners, making it inhospitable and wet. The solution for Maximus, which Othello never finds, is to let the waters in and remake once-stable meanings into something more fluid. Looking at the sea means being bounded by something you cannot understand. Olson turns this insight into a maxim: "Love the world – and stay inside it!" The intermingling of ocean and human never becomes comfortable, but it does not lead to murder.

The sea-storm in *Othello* creates a crisis of meaning that hastens the play's insistent drive toward violence. The immediate narrative resolution of the storm, however, mirrors neither Maximus's acceptance of the sea's destabilizing intimacy with the land nor Lucretius's Stoic ju-jitsu, in which the ocean's violence stimulates reason's victory over the fear of death. Instead, the Venetian survivors transform the near-disaster into a familiar early modern maritime story, the arrival of a treasure galleon. After describing Othello's ship as "stoutly timbered" (2.1.48) and properly piloted, Cassio imagines Desdemona as the magical cargo that ensures its own passage. "Tempests themselves," he rhapsodizes, "do omit / Their mortal natures, letting go safely by / The divine Desdemona" (2.1.68, 71–3). In retrospect, and in the context of this play, the dangers of the voyage seem sexual more than maritime. The confusion of sea and sky takes on erotic coloring. Montano's question, "But, good lieutenant, is your general wived?" (2.1.60), may imply that a rumor from Venice has outrun the storm, but the shift of attention from naval warfare to domestic entanglements also matches the play's dramatic structure. Desdemona, whom Iago has already described (in maritime language) as a "land carrack" (1.2.50) and, if "fast married" (1.2.11), a "lawful prize" (1.2.51), arrives on Cyprus as if born, like Venus, from the foamy sea. The portrait Cassio constructs of Othello's subsequent arrival is distinctly sexualized:

> Great Jove, Othello guard,
> And swell his sail with thine own powerful breath
> That he may bless this bay with his tall ship,
> Make love's quick pants in Desdemona's arms,
> Give renewed fire to our extincted spirits
> And bring all Cyprus comfort!"
>
> (2.1.77–82)

Cassio's erotic imagination, with its vision of Othello's "tall ship" and swelled sails, the image of Desdemona as a fertile bay, and the hope that the biracial match would give "renewed fire" to Venice's stale aristocracy all suggest a different way to socialize the sexual sea. Cassio's "sweet union" of Moor and Venetian counters Iago's "beast with two backs" (1.1.115). If Iago had not already commandeered the sea as his own private signal, the "sweet pants" of Othello's arrival at Cyprus might have presided over a happier play.

Iago's Not

in! in! the bow-spirit, bird, the beak
in, the bend is, in, goes in, the form

> *that which you make, what holds, which is*
> *the law of object, strut after strut, what you are,*
> > *what you must be, what*
> *the force can throw up, can, right now hereinafter erect,*
> *the mast, the mast, the tender*
> *mast!*
>
> > > (*Charles Olson*, The Maximus Poems)

In its opacity, the sea in *Othello* has its own God, or rather its anti-God: Iago. We've ignored this figure's oceanic context for too long. Editors have long noted Iago's maritime vocabulary, which includes terms like compass, salt, carrack, cable, prize, fathom, and sail, but critics have not recognized how deeply maritime this character is. While not a voyager like Pericles or a shipwreck survivor like Egeon, Iago's restless nihilism carries more than a whiff of salt. His pattern of negation, the opacity and mutability that fool his wife and his general, matches the ocean's unstable nature. "I am not what I am" (1.1.64) says the ancient, famously echoing God's voice to Moses (Exodus 3:14). His nihilistic "not" is the seaman's knot with which he manipulates his general. (His "not" also echoes Viola in *Twelfth Night*, another figure whose connection with the sea has been under-estimated.) Against the stable landfall of Othello's poetic music, Iago sounds maritime discord in ragged prose. Even Lodovico, the Venetian aristocrat who arrives late to Cyprus and attempts to salvage some order from the last scene's bloody bedroom, recognizes that Iago resembles the great waters; he describes the captured villain as "More fell than anguish, hunger, or the sea" (5.2.360). Reading *Othello* as a maritime play means taking ship with Iago.

This character, whose name and one epithet ("diablo," 2.3.157) link him to Spain, the greatest seagoing empire of the early seventeenth century, advertises his connection to the maritime world in a collection of epithets and phrases. Especially early in the play, Iago scatters sailor-talk liberally; he refers to "scurvy and provoking terms" (1.2.8), asks Othello if he is "fast married" (i.e., tied fast, 1.2.11), and suggests that the law of Venice will give Brabantio "cable" (1.2.17) to draw Othello back. He links himself to Roderigo "with cables of perdurable toughness" (1.3.338–9). He habitually imagines himself as a ship, at first "be-leed and calmed" (1.1.29) by Cassio's ascension to lieutenancy, and then subsequently "sail[ing] freely" as his plans on Cyprus develop (2.3.60). He even uses Ariel's maritime word to indicate Venice's absolute dependence on Othello: "Another of his fathom have they none" (1.1.150). Some of his obscure witticisms, like his joke about changing "the cod's head for the salmon's tail" (2.1.155), turn on watery figures. Iago's salt-language forms a half-hidden pattern around him. The sea, itself mysterious, may not clarify his motives, but it epitomizes his power.

Iago's maritime vocabulary underlines his opacity and his ability to reshape himself at every moment. In addition to his habitual references to sexual "salt," another key maritime term for Iago is "compass," a word that in Shakespeare's lifetime was shifting meanings as it came more frequently to identify the essential tool for finding out direction at sea. In Shakespeare's plays, however, "compass" never refers directly to the navigational instrument. The word appears in different forms five times in *Othello*, by a slight margin the most in any play of Shakespeare's. On a symbolic level "compassing" – encircling or bringing to completion – is precisely what Iago prevents: Othello cannot grasp his fortune because, thanks to Iago, he loses track of where he is. Though his seamanlike language suggests that Iago has some experience of navigation, compassing for him always implies sexual embrace. He insists that Roderigo will be "compassing thy joy" (1.3.361) if he follows Iago's advice, and he later employs a doubly maritime metaphor when describing Cassio's supposed desire for Desdemona: he says the lieutenant wants to be "compassing of his salt" (2.1.238). That Iago should invoke the haven-finding tool of the compass only in a sexual sense contrasts with Othello's use of the word as a span of time (the sibyl who sewed his handkerchief numbered "two hundred compasses" [3.4.73] before doomsday) and the Clown's and Roderigo's conventional uses of it to signify human understanding ("the compass of a man's wit," 3.4.21; "within reason and compass" 4.2.221). Iago's compass, like his salt, increases human sexual desires but provides no structures for ordering them. Iago's focalizing energy – his "now, now, very now!" (1.1.87) – rejects the slow progress of orderly narrative in favor of the instant of desire. Like the sea, he changes constantly. Even when he invokes his dependence on "dilatory time" (2.3.368), his scene-ending soliloquies attempt to control each instant of the plot.

Iago as anti-God of the sea exploits the dissolving force of salt water rather than the technical labors of seafaring men. His sea embodies lust and disorder, in which wine in "flowing cups" (2.3.55) breaks Cassio's reputation and transforms Desdemona's "virtue into pitch" (2.3.355). All that is solid melts, but into liquid not air. Like the sailors whose language he borrows, Iago works "by wit and not by witchcraft" (2.3.367), and he insists that his tools can reorder his world. Iago presents himself as mastermind and improvisational artist, and it's noteworthy that his early hymn to self-sufficiency operates in a landed context. When he imagines human bodies "as gardens, to the which our will are gardeners" (1.3.320–1), the land-centered image implies an Iago who cherishes life on shore. His insistence that Roderigo talk "no more of drowning" (1.3.378) extends this purported rejection of water. But longing for dry land and stability seems just a mask to gull Iago's fool and purse; Iago's heart remains unknowable precisely because it lies, metaphorically, in the deep sea.

Othello's Constancy

The salmon of
wisdom when,
ecstatically, one
leaps into the Beloved's
love. And feels the air
*   enter into*

strike into one's previously breathing
system
> (*Charles Olson*, The Maximus Poems)

Against Iago's salt "not," Othello's generalship appears overmatched. It's not that he lacks experience of the watery world. His military command, after all, is the Venetian fleet, and his career includes "moving accidents by flood and field" (1.3.136). But looking closely at his actions, both the retrospective "story of my life" (1.3.130) and the events in the play, reveals a man who craves constancy. Not only does he prefer dry ground beneath his feet, he also adds solidity to his own maritime history. His rhapsody upon his safe arrival on Cyprus establishes his belief that water is an evil to be endured, not a mystery to be explored:

> O my soul's joy,
> If after every tempest come such calms
> May the winds blow until they have wakened death,
> And let the labouring bark climb hills of seas,
> Olympus-high, and duck again as low
> As hell's from heaven. If it were now to die
> 'Twere to be most happy, for I fear
> My soul hath her content so absolute
> That not another comfort like to this
> Succeeds in unknown fate.
>
> (2.1.182–91)

This passage shows Othello's familiarity with the classical and biblical heaven/hell topos, and it also shows him craving the calms that follow storms. Unlike Lucretius, Othello finds nothing in the storm worth his attention. He sees only his "fair warrior" (2.1.180). His description of the storm, in another familiar topos, turns the roiling waters into landed "hills." Like Shakespeare's humanist culture, Othello carefully balances references to classical literature (Olympus, "unknown fate") and Christianity ("my soul" twice). His longing for a quick death, signaled by grammatical ellipsis ("If it were now to die . . ."), shows him rushing past both Lucretian philosophy and the Psalmist's awe to embrace death in place of the sea. The stability he longs for – content, comfort, replacing the unknown with the known – indicates his basic desire for land instead of sea.

Othello's aversion to liquid disorder structurally opposes Iago's sea-infused chaos. As early as his first scene, Othello's language resists liquefaction. In a formulation that limns his fear of sexuality, he tells Iago that were it not for his love of "the gentle Desdemona," he would not his "unhoused free condition / Put into circumscription and confine / For the sea's worth" (1.2.25–8). His fear of being housed, circumscribed, and confined gets juxtaposed against an external "sea's worth," a foreign space of "rich and strange" treasures. This vast, mercantile ocean supports Othello's heroic sense of self, as does the storm that sinks the Turkish fleet, but it doesn't penetrate his character. Like sexuality, perhaps, it's valuable, but it's not his. (Iago's insistent connection between sex and the sea colors this passage uncomfortably.) Later in the same scene Othello emphasizes the force of water to corrupt male potency: "Keep up your bright swords," he says to a brawling crowd, "for the dew will rust them" (1.2.59). Like other warrior heroes, Othello represents himself as a sword, and as such he fears water. His resistance to water continues in his madness; he eschews liquid poison (4.1.201–5), and later justifies killing Desdemona because "She was false as water" (5.2.132). He is, as Desdemona knows, a product of "the sun where he was born" (3.4.30), and she recognizes the impact of jealousy on him in strikingly liquid terms: "Something . . . / Hath puddled his clear spirit" (3.4.141, 144). Even the fatal handkerchief, talisman of Othello's marriage, is, at a basic level, a tool for sopping up excess liquid. When all efforts to keep dry fail, Othello's fantasy of a constant life deserts him. Once water does its work – dew rusts him, puddles muddy him, the sea disorients him – Othello loses himself.

Liquefaction overwhelms Othello in the play's final acts. He "foams at mouth" (4.1.154) in his madness, and near the end of the long scene in which Iago activates his jealousy, he fixates on the liquid consequences of his revenge: "O blood, blood, blood" (3.3.454). Even more than blood, however, tears unman Othello, first Desdemona's ("Proceed you in your tears," he says, 4.1.256) and then his own:

> Had it pleased heaven
> To try me with affliction, had they rained
> All kinds of sores and shames on my bare head
> Steeped me in poverty to the very lips
> Given to captivity me and my utmost hopes,
> I should have found in some place of my soul
> A drop of patience; but, alas, to make me
> The fixed figure for the time of scorn
> To point his slow and moving finger at!
> Yet could I bear that too, well, very well:
> But there where I have garnered up my heart,
> Where either I must live or bear no life,
> The fountain from the which my current runs
> Or else dries up – to be discarded thence!
> Or keep it as a cistern for foul toads
> To knot and gender in!
>
>   (4.2.48–63)

Water courses through these lines: rained, steeped, drop, fountain, current, dries up, cistern. Unlike the clear conflict between dew and bright swords, these images articulate a more complex symbolic pattern, in which certain kinds of fresh water – fountains, currents – seem essential to Othello, and Desdemona has become their source. He now fears drought as well as rust and flood. But even in the first half of this speech, where his "drop of patience" opposes itself to the rain of "sores and shames" from heaven, Othello's resistance to watery inconstancy remains. He recognizes that Desdemona (like Venice) represents a combination of land and water, and that mixture unsettles him even as he craves it. Like Maximus of Gloucester's "salmon of / wisdom," Othello leaps "ecstatically" into his love's arms, and his system ruptures when plunged into a foreign element.

At the heart of Othello's marriage and his tragedy lie a poetic attempt to transform the sea from Iago's realm of shifting desires into a place of heroic constancy. This hero from the land of the sun, the catalog of whose adventures provides a tour of classical deserts via Herodotus and Pliny, marries into maritime Venice but wants to solidify its watery world. He longs for clear fountains but gets a salt sea. He's still voicing his hostility to water at the play's end when he describes suicide as a "sea-mark" that fixes his "utmost sail" (5.2.266) and when he insists that he is "unused to the melting mood" (5.2.347). But his most drastic attempt to embrace the sea while denying its nature comes in the middle of the play. When Iago suggests that Othello's mind (like the sea) "perhaps may change," the general counters:

> Never, Iago. Like to the Pontic sea
> Whose icy current and compulsive course
> Ne'er keeps retiring ebb but keeps due on
> To the Propontic and the Hellespont:
> Even so my bloody thoughts with violent pact
> Shall ne'er look back, ne'er ebb to humble love . . .
>
> (3.3.456–61)

The purported consistency of the current exiting the Black Sea toward the Mediterranean fascinated early geographers (Shakespeare adapts Philemon Holland's translation of Pliny), but Othello's larger fantasy here remakes the sea, emblem of inconstancy and change, into a constant stream. Othello sees this radically atypical sea as an emblem of his heroic self. He too wishes to be "icy . . . and compulsive," to never retire but keep "due on," and to never "ebb to humble love." Othello's repetition of "ne'er . . . ebb" suggests that he, like the Pontic current, will never flow freely like ordinary water. (His opposite, here and elsewhere, is Antony, who at times embraces liquidity: "Let Rome in Tiber melt . . ." 1.1.34.) Othello's failure to keep his solidity matched against Iago's facility with the sea translates this play's domestic tragedy into an allegory of humanity's relationship with land and sea. The play figures a fork for early modern England poised on the cusp of maritime empire. Spain, treachery, the sea, and Iago? Or classical Africa, constancy, land, and doomed Othello?

Iago without Words

> *It is undone business*
> *I speak of, this morning,*
> *with the sea*
> *stretching out*
> *from my feet.*
>   ("*Maximus*, to himself")

Iago's closing silence spits one last time in the face of psychological realism, as the "motiveless malignancy" refuses to explain himself. The play won't tell us what he's thinking. If, however, we associate Iago's nihilism, his embrace of being "not that I am," with a symbolic choosing of the sea over the land and water over earth, these lines acquire a slightly different resonance. "Demand me nothing," Iago says, "What you know, you know. / From this time forth I never will speak word" (5.2.299–300). At this moment, Iago resembles the sea. He no longer speaks the language of mariners who work on the waves, but instead represents the ocean as such: wordless, malign, opaque, amoral. His final lines vary the biblical cadences of his opening self-definition. Now that "I am not that I am" has modulated into "What you know, you know," the evacuation of Iago's humanity has become complete. He stretches out before us, at our mercy but finally untouchable. Iago's manipulative power lies miniaturized in these two resonant lines. The first phrase, "I am not that I am," uses negation as a poison to infect existing value systems (leading to such false warnings as "O beware, my lord, of jealousy!" 3.3.167). The second, "What you know, you know," encourages his general's suppositions to harden into facts (as he suggests to Othello, "Will you think so?" 4.1.1). In his final silence, Iago abandons the language he has done so much to corrupt and assumes the wordless stance of the sea: violent, distant, uninterpretable. His business is done, but, like Maximus on the rocky Massachusetts shoreline, he leaves us contemplating "the sea / stretching out / from my feet." He's of the world, but not our world. From creatures like these, it's not only words that move us.

Sunken Treasure

What pain is it, to go down, like Jonah, all the way? What do the waters want? What's at the bottom?

At the surface the world breaks. Columns of air shatter into devilish brilliance and beauty. You're out, then you're in: no middle ground.

First the riches of upper ocean, boundless fields of ripe and golden wheat. Everything we love is here, swimming, flashing, tumbling, cradling bodies, and refracting light. Here Noah's flood never subsides, here is world without end or limit. All subtle and submarine. Look into the fish's eyes, and you see – nothing. No strange analogy to something in yourself.

Passing five full fathoms colors darken and grow heavy. The ribs and terrors of the whale press down. Monsters swim, fast and fearful. No place to stay.

They wink up at us from the depths, skulls with be-gemmed eye-sockets, wedges of gold, encrusted anchors, heaps of pearl. Fish-gnawed men and what's become of a thousand fearful wracks. Treasures of the slimy bottom. Captives of the envious flood. What we're looking for.

What's there? Not just gold and death-fragments, not even pearls whose price we spent long since. The sea's floor hides a universal cannibalism, a full awfulness, a two-stranded lesson. Here went Jonah, ten thousand fathoms down, weeds wrapped about his head, and all the watery world of woe bowled over him. Here Prospero's book lies mudded. Here God-fugitives reach a place beyond rest.

Two things. The real and final face of our world. And the limit of what we can imagine touching.

Bursting back to air and light, we sing what we can and sell the rest, remembering what we can't salvage.

No insular Tahiti.

Chapter 3

Swimming: *The Comedy of Errors*

Pip saw the multitudinous, God-omnipresent, coral insects, that out of the firmament of waters heaved the colossal orbs. He saw God's foot on the treadle of the loom, and spoke it; and therefore his shipmates called him mad. So man's insanity is heaven's sense; and wandering from all mortal reason, man comes at last to that celestial thought, which, to reason, is absurd and frantic; and weal or woe, feels then uncompromised, indifferent as his God.

(Moby-Dick)

Nothing works like immersion. The sea touches human bodies most intimately through the halting and laborious art of swimming. We know it when we're in it – or at least we feel like we know it. Depictions of swimming expose the awkward fit between human bodies and the ocean. It's impossible to know what kind of swimmer Shakespeare himself was, growing up on the Avon river. Recreational swimming was still exotic in Elizabethan England, like other Continental arts, and it was even banned at Cambridge in 1571. Literary images, like Spenser's knights in full armor jousting mid-stream (*The Faerie Queene*, 5.2.16–17), suggest that many poets had little practical experience with the water. Interest seems to have grown in the late sixteenth century: the Cambridge humanist Everard Digby published a Latin instructional treatise *De Arte Natandi* in 1587, and Christopher Middleton Englished it in 1595. But in Shakespeare's plays immersion is less often a call to swim than a threat to survival. Compared to other mammals – the primary biblical and Shakespearean example is Leviathan – humans are poor swimmers. We cannot go out far, and we cannot go in deep, to adapt Robert Frost's language. Going into the water means encountering the world's raw, wet hostility.

The difficulties of swimming underlie the world's inhospitality in Shakespeare's plays. Being in the water calls up a vision of human insufficiency, as in *Macbeth*'s "spent swimmers, that do cling together / And choke their art" (1.2.8–9), or of failed heroism, as when Caesar dares Cassius to swim the "angry flood" (*Julius Caesar*, 1.2.103). The most resonant of Shakespeare's swimmers is condemned Egeon, whose name echoes the Aegean Sea. His play spirals out from the near-fatal immersion that scatters his family across the eastern Mediterranean. This early play invokes the sea in multiple contexts; the waters are a space of transformation (linked to Circe's cup and witchcraft), a site of loss (for Egeon, Emilia, and their family), a vehicle for commerce (for the merchants), and a source of long-deferred rescue and reunion at the end. Like the salt-drenched late plays *Pericles* and *The Tempest*, *The Comedy of Errors* presents a romance-inflected split image of the waters, which first threaten destruction (1.1) but then resolve into salvation (5.1). As Shakespeare's earliest experiment with the sea-plot he adapted from *The Odyssey* and Greek romance, *The Comedy of Errors* presents his first sustained focus on what the ocean does to human bodies. Being in the sea creates submission, loss, and unexpected wisdom. The treasures Egeon and his family find in the ocean aren't pearls but a fatalism born of recognizing human finitude in the infinite sea.

Alongside Egeon swim the stories of many sailors whose ships fail them, starting with Jonah and Odysseus and Aeneas. Shipwreck remains one of Western culture's most enduring literary symbols, as recent novels such as Yann Martel's *Life of Pi* (2001) and Günter Grass's *Crabwalk* (2002) show. Later in his career, Shakespeare would split the swimming survivor into passive floaters like Viola and active strivers like her brother Sebastian. This division informs the two other swimmers that this chapter ranges alongside Egeon, Ferdinand,

and Trinculo from *The Tempest*. But to recover the full strangeness and intensity of Egeon's immersion, I first turn to Melville.

Pip's Indifference

Moby-Dick teems with swimmers, human and not, and swimming itself becomes a divine attribute when the white whale arrives for the chase that ends the novel: "not Jove, that great majesty Supreme! did surpass the glorified White Whale as he so divinely swam" (409). Swimming makes the whale godlike, but human swimmers encounter their limits more harshly. The cabin-boy Pip, who "loved life" but was "gloomy-jolly" (319), falls into Egeon's place, stranded in deep waters. Melville's variation of the ancient shipwreck topos emphasizes the terror of immersion. Pip swims in a theological vastness, a more-than-human immensity that, as it maddens him, reveals the kind of visions that Egeon stoically ignores. Pressed into service in the whale-boat, Pip twice leaps into the ocean in fear. After cutting his line and losing the whale the first time, Stubb abandons the cabin-boy: "Pip was left behind on the sea, like a hurried traveler's trunk . . . It was a beautiful, bounteous, blue day; the spangled sea calm and cool, and flatly stretching away, all round, to the horizon, like gold-beater's skin hammered out to the extremest. Bobbing up and down in that sea, Pip's ebon head showed like a head of cloves" (321). Unlike Egeon's stormy Mediterranean, Pip's ocean shows a tranquil face; Melville's language invokes pastoral fantasies of harmony with a nature that provides bounty, beauty, and calm. Pip's head of cloves makes him part of a bucolic scene, and the simile of the gold-beater's skin suggests a working-together of different natural materials (in this case, ox intestine and gold leaf) to create beauty. Only the first metaphor, of the errant traveler's trunk, recalls the now-distant world of humankind. But that wandering voyager is long gone, and Pip's new destination isn't at all human.

Alone in the "shoreless ocean," abandoned to "heartless immensity" (321), Pip epitomizes swimming in its raw state. He reminds us that humans aren't good swimmers. He keeps himself afloat – "in calm weather, to swim in the open ocean is as easy to the practised swimmer as to ride in a spring-carriage ashore" (321) – but falls into an "intense concentration of self" (321). The solitary swimmer encounters the God-sea of the ancient world, full of "multitudinous, God-omnipresent coral insects" that break and remake his mind. He gets rescued by the Pequod, "by the merest chance" (321), but not before he has exchanged human for divine sense. Pip's madness creates a new attitude toward the sea. He ends up with neither Ahab's rage nor Ishmael's obsessive curiosity; he neither fears the sea like Othello nor learns from it like Lucretius's philosopher. Rather, the hostile sea generates "celestial thought" and makes Pip "indifferent as his God." Deep in the watery world, he ceases to care about land, or self, or white whale. This abstraction of self, this alienation from things in the world, is swimming's wisdom. Like Egeon, Pip's dead while living.

Egeon's Loss

Surviving Pip's fate, Egeon represents what the waters cannot drown. At the opening of the play, he treats immersion as a rhetorical challenge: he claims not to know how to "speak my griefs unspeakable" (1.1.32). Despite his sense that language fails him, his report from the depths – his attempt to tell what Pip cannot – dominates the play's first scene. He opens with a couplet (1.1.1–2), replies to the Duke with a second couplet (1.1.26–7), narrates his story in three long set-pieces (1.1.31–95, 98–120, 124–39), and ends the scene with a third couplet (1.1.157–8). He speaks in 107 of the scene's 158 lines, about 68 percent, and then disappears until 5.1. His rhetoric lacks Ariel's musicality or Iago's negative bite, but the story of his life (unlike Othello's) showcases the impact of the sea on human bodies. Early in his tale, he explains that his crisis was "wrought by nature, not by vile offence" (1.1.34), emphasizing that shipwreck, as he understands it, represents the natural condition of humanity in the world.

Shakespeare adapts the familiar religious trope of mortal life as a shipwreck from a tradition that begins with biblical texts like the Book of Jonah and includes early modern works like Edmund Pet's *Lamentable News* (1613), John King's sermons on Jonah (1594), and Thomas Jackson's theological essay *The Raging Tempest Still'd* (1623). These works in turn invoke a tradition of Patristic commentary that derives from Augustine's *De Beata Vida*. In this tradition, the sea's rage reveals the naked majesty of God. Egeon, however, treats the ocean as more natural than divine. In this he anticipates developing strains of proto-scientific thought like Francis Bacon's experimentalism and the hydrographical writings of William Gilbert, William Bourne, and others. These two traditions, the religious and the hydrographical, developed intertwined with each other. Shakespeare's Egeon anticipates emerging connections between God's power and empirical observation that would undergird "natural theology" in the eighteenth century.

Egeon's patient empiricism recalls many portraits of practical seamanship in early modern literature, including the Boatswain in *The Tempest*, but maritime labor cannot save this shipwreck victim. His ship's crew betrays him; the mariners steal the lifeboat and abandon their passengers: "The sailors sought safety by our boat / And left the ship, then sinking-ripe, to us" (1.1.76–7). Alone in the "always-wind-obeying deep" (1.1.63), Egeon and Emilia arrange their two sets of twins symbolically: "My wife . . . fasten'd him [i.e., Antipholus of Ephesus] unto a small spare mast, / Such as sea-faring men provide for storms; To him one of the other twins [i.e., Dromio of Ephesus] was bound / Whilst I had been like heedful of the other" (1.1.78–82). The description resembles the so-called spar rescue topos, in which shipwreck survivors cling to jagged fragments of spars or masts, that would become popular in both the literary tradition that descended from Virgil and the pictorial tradition that Dutch maritime artists such as the van de Veldes brought to England in the seventeenth century. While not a realistic portrait (masts did regularly go by the board, but seldom split into picturesque fragments), the spar rescue symbolizes the failure of human technology in rough seas. The fragment on which the survivors float is all that stands between them and the full immersion that drives Pip insane. The spar rescue reduces social bonds to a minimal, fragmentary structure. Two sets of three people – a parent, a child, and an orphan – sit "at either end the mast" (1.1.85), abandoned to fate, "obedient to the stream" (1.1.86). Alone like Pip on opaque waters, this symmetrical family – whose mirror-structures generate the "errors" of the play's middle acts – shows human bodies and communities at the mercy of the sea.

Egeon's family doesn't receive Pip's multitudinous visions; they instead see a world become ocean: alienating, threatening, and vast. Faced with immersion, Egeon learns to survive the Aegean through patience and a deep fatalism. He sees a maritime nature nearly as incomprehensible as Pip's, but he never looks for God in those waters. Instead, nature and society rescue him together. The mist and storm eventually clears – "at length the sun, gazing upon the earth, / Dispers'd those vapours that offended us, / And by the benefit of his wished light / The seas wax'd calm" (1.1.88–91) – and the family returns to the human world, through "Two ships . . . Of Corinth that, of Epidarus this" (1.1.92–3). Before these classical polities can rescue them, however, they "were encounter'd by a mighty rock," which "splitted [us] in the midst" and cause "this unjust divorce of us" (1.1.103–4). The rock, emerging unexpectedly amid the waters, divides the family and seals Egeon's tragedy (which he blames on "Fortune" 1.1.105). Building the wreck upon a rock initiates the series of motifs that give Shakespeare's Plautine play Christian resonance, including moving the setting from Epidamnum to Ephesus, making Emilia an Abbess, and seeding the dialogue with Christian language ("Satan avoid," says the Syracusan Antipholus, 4.3.46). Egeon's frame-tale, which derives from Latin miracle tales like *Apollonius of Tyre* and Greek romance as well as biblical narratives like St. Paul's shipwreck on Malta, emphasizes the enduring mystery of the natural world, especially the sea. Swimming teaches fatalism, and also hunger for revelation.

The play's urban middle acts, while not presenting the ocean directly, use watery images to echo and extend Egeon's maritime lament. Moisture facilitates Ephesian transformative magic, especially in the "mist" (2.2.216) that the Syracusan Antipholus sees in the city. Water's natural magic also subtends Luciana's role as "sweet mermaid" (3.2.45, 163), a purified version of the Homeric sirens to whom the Syracusan Antipholus connects her (3.2.47). But water does not threaten this play's characters as in *Othello*. Water in Ephesus is not apocalyptic; it notably fails in a domestic chore, cleaning the grease off Nell's complexion; "Noah's flood could not do it" (3.2.104–5), protests the Syracusan Dromio. The offstage presence of the eastern Mediterranean creates a dense mercantile network, its seaways linking Syracuse, Ephesus, Corinth, Epidarus, and other cities. Especially in the last two acts, when the Syracusan Antipholus is "bound to sea" (4.1.33) and his oft-mentioned departure threatens to preempt the disentanglement of the plot, the sea's transport-facilitating role underlies the play's incessant mobility.

Two famous speeches in *The Comedy of Errors* invoke water's paradigmatic role as metaphor for unstable identity. Both the Syracusan Antipholus and Adriana imagine themselves as drops of water in a massive ocean, and each, in slightly different ways, finds this image destabilizing. Like Pip, they lose themselves in the sea. Mourning the loss of his family, the Syracusan Antipholus sees the ocean as an over-identity, a massive containing wholeness that frustrates his ability to know himself:

> I to the world am like a drop of water
> That in the ocean seeks to find another drip,
> Who, falling there to find his fellow forth,
> (Unseen, inquisitive) confounds himself.
> So I, to find a mother and a brother,
> In quest of them, unhappy, lose myself.
>
> (1.2.35–40)

The ocean's flexibility, the physical unity between any one drop and the whole sea, "confounds" Antipholus because it simultaneously defines him and frustrates definition. When he looks closely at the ocean, he (like Pip) ends up lost. The cascading f-alliteration ("falling . . . find his fellow forth") anticipates Ariel's "full fathom five . . . father." These sound-chains invoke the inarticulate music of the sea, which hints at wordless profundity but never pronounces it. In the sea of this play – a warmer, more hospitable place than the war-torn sea of *Othello*, to say nothing of the flooded England of *King Lear* – individual identities don't last long.

When Adriana, thinking the Syracusan Antipholus is her husband, turns this sea-language on him, she remakes the sea as a metaphor for the marriage bed. "For know, my love," she says,

> as easy mayst thou fall
> A drop of water in the breaking gulf,
> And take unmingled thence that drop again
> Without addition or diminishing,
> As take from me thyself, and not me too.
>
> (2.2.125–29)

Aligning the human unity of marriage, in which Adriana is "thy dear self's better part" (2.2.123), with the anonymity of drops in the "breaking gulf," she celebrates the loss of self that the Syracusan Antipholus defines in metaphor and Egeon in narrative. Adriana anticipates Iago's and Viola's negations – "I am not Adriana," she says, "nor thy wife" (2.2.112) – but she pleads that her husband join her in an all-embracing sea. At the comedy's center, two landlocked women – Adriana who find unity in the waters, and Luciana the misidentified "mermaid" – provide chains that finally anchor this maritime family in Ephesus. These women's refusal of sea travel, which contrasts sharply with Desdemona's fatal embrace of it, creates a pattern in which domestic concerns – marriages, kitchens, even paying bills – provide buffers against the shock of immersion.

Fighting the Water

Anyone who's ever taught a child to swim knows that fighting the water doesn't work. As early modern European culture worked through what the French critic Alain Corbin calls the "repulsion" typical of biblical and classical images of the sea, swimming was often depicted as a struggle. From Beowulf's night-contest against Brecca and the sea-monsters to Odysseus's harrowing landfall on Phaiacia, Western literary culture treats the sea as a hostile environment. From this point of view, Egeon's fatalistic detachment, his resignation to the embrace of the sea that names him, represents the relaxation into a foreign element that makes swimming possible. Egeon's narrative shows Shakespeare groping toward what Melville would explore in *Moby-Dick*, the utopian fantasy of a fully maritime human. In Shakespeare's plays, however, Egeon's partial accommodation with the sea remains a minority position. The clearest example of the opposite attitude, in which water must always be fought, comes in the description of Ferdinand swimming to shore in *The Tempest*. Speaking to the King, Francisco suggests that Ferdinand's combat with the waves was so intense that he may have survived:

> Sir, he may live.
> I saw him beat the surges under him
> And ride upon their backs. He trod the water,
> Whose enmity he flung aside, and breasted
> The surge most swoll'n that met him. His bold head
> 'Bove the contentious waves he kept and oared
> Himself with his good arms in lusty stroke
> To th'shore, that o'er his wave-worn basis bowed
> As stooping to relieve him. I doubt not
> He came alive to land.

$$(2.1.114–23)$$

A cascade of active, transitive verbs – beat, ride, trod, breasted, oared – define Ferdinand's combat with the water. Francisco even imagines that rescue must come from "th'shore" and its "wave-worn basis" of cliffs, which bow as if to aid the prince. Some features of the language derive from Virgil's depiction of the sea-serpents who assail Laöcoon (*Aeneid* 2.203–8), which further suggests that, to Italian courtiers at least, the sea is a treacherous foe in epic combat.

Egeon's contrasting case suggests that Shakespeare imagined other attitudes besides Ferdinand's death-struggle against the waves. (In fact, we might wonder how reliable Francisco's report is; Ferdinand's actions after immersion – sitting and weeping – don't emphasize conflict.) In *The Tempest*, swimming can be painful – Prospero forces Ariel "to tread the ooze / Of the salt deep" (1.2.253) – but it is safe, at least inside the charmed circle of the magic island. The clown Trinculo's description of his landfall inverts Ferdinand's struggle. He describes swimming as neither combat nor resignation, but a harmonious imitation of nature. Answering Stephano's question about how he made it to shore, Trinculo quips, "Swum ashore, man, like a duck. I can swim like a duck, I'll be sworn" (2.2.125–6). It sounds like a comic throw-away line (and often is, in performance), but the underlying fantasy that humans can be as aquatic as marine animals counteracts Francisco's language of oceanic struggle. Like the violent storm that only appears to threaten the ship in *The Tempest*'s opening scene, Trinculo's perspective makes swimming less dangerous than it seems.

Queequeg as Aquaman

A more comprehensive vision of a maritime human – we might call it the aquaman fantasy – doesn't get fully articulated in Shakespeare's plays. Trinculo swims well, but he's just a clown. The only other semi-positive portrait of human swimming comes in Wosley's reference to "little wanton boys that swim on bladders, / . . . far beyond [their] depth" (*King Henry 8*, 3.2.359–61), and the bladders emphasize that the boys can't swim very well. (Leviathans and spirits like

Ariel do better.) As Melville plumbs the maritime "wonder-world," however, his novel completes this fantasy of marine humanity in the figure of Queequeg, noble savage and "George Washington cannibalistically developed." As a radical extension of the sea-man that Egeon never quite becomes, "this sea Prince of Wales" represents a perfectly harmonious relationship between humanity and ocean. Where Egeon imagines the sea as unfathomable and immersion makes him resign to Fortune, Queequeg rescues less-powerful fellow mariners from the depths. He does it by diving straight in.

Queequeg pulls two characters from the sea in *Moby-Dick*, a greenhorn on the boat to Nantucket, and Tashtego when he falls into a dead whale's head. These episodes portray the heroic cannibal, loosely based on Melville's encounters with South Sea islanders and printed descriptions of New Zealanders, as at home in the water in a way that most humans never are. When swimming after the sunken greenhorn, Queequeg, like Trinculo, resembles an animal: "For three minutes or more he was seen swimming like a dog, throwing his long arms straight out before him, and by turns revealing his brawny shoulder through the freezing foam." Ishmael's appreciation of Queequeg's physical beauty, and the juxtaposition of brawny body and freezing foam, gesture toward an impossible union of man and sea. Queequeg's abilities, however, are not limited to swimming; he can also see through the water when others cannot. "I looked at the grand and glorious fellow," Ishmael continues, "but saw no one to be saved." These same waters, however, aren't opaque to the cannibal: "Shooting himself perpendicularly from the water, Queequeg now took an instant's glance around him, and seeming to see just how matters were, dived down and disappeared." At the bottom of his ocean, Queequeg finds and rescues the greenhorn. "Was there ever such unconsciousness?" rhapsodizes Ishmael, emphasizing that Queequeg represents a purely physical, not intellectual, relationship to the sea. An idealized masculine hero, Queequeg creates a relationship with the sea that avoids Ishmael's own intellectual fantasies, pedantry, and mortal fear. Speaking an awkward pidgin and making only a mark when called to sign the ship's papers, the cannibal represents everything that bookish Ishmael (and Melville) is not.

After the first rescue establishes Queequeg as Ishmael's ideal partner, the second transforms the whale fishery itself into a salt water baptism. The second recovery suggests that even master mariners remain at risk, as the harpooner Tashtego, gathering spermaceti oil out of a whale's head, "dropped head-foremost down into this great Tun of Heidelburgh, and with a horribly oily gurgling, went clean out of sight!" Never one to undersell his metaphors, Ishmael describes "the lifeless head throbbing and heaving just below the surface of the sea, as if that moment seized with some momentous idea." This symbolic water-birth, with its echo of Athena springing from Zeus's head, threatens to engulf Tashtego, the Gay Head native who, atop the mainmast, eventually becomes the last casualty of the sinking Pequod. His near-death shows the ocean overcoming even the most apparently maritime humans. If Tashtego, a natural product of coastal New England, resembles a Trinculo-style temporary accommodation with the sea, his rescuer displays a fully aquatic, more-than-human affinity for water. After "brave Queequeg had dived to the rescue" (271), "his keen sword" performs a Caesarian birth, accomplishing "the deliverance, or rather, delivery, of Tashtego." The second rescue extends Queequeg's mastery of the sea: the first dive into murky depths represents an aggressive penetration of the sea, but the second shows him as midwife, carefully manipulating "poor Tash" so as to draw him "forth in the good old way – head foremost." These paired episodes reconfigure the two kinds of swimming that *The Tempest* presents via Ferdinand and Trinculo: first, an aggressive dive in, and second, a more subtle working-together.

Queequeg's utopian affinity with the sea cannot save him, but the Kokovokan prince does rescue Ishmael, his friend and "joint-stock" partner. Melville kills his aquaman, but Ishmael's desperate longing for the waters, his passion for "all rivers and oceans," abides. At the novel's end, Ishmael assumes Egeon's position. Having being thrown out of Ahab's whaleboat (like Pip out of Stubb's), Ishmael watches the death-match between whale and Pequod while "floating on the margin." After the ship goes down, the "coffin life-buoy" shoots up from the center of the vortex to save him. The life-buoy, made from the coffin for which Queequeg had been measured when he lay sick of fever, recreates something like Queequeg's magical harmony with the waters for Ishmael's solitary float: "for almost one whole day and night, I floated on a soft and dirge-like main. The unharming sharks, they glided by as if with padlocks on their mouths; the savage sea-hawks sailed with sheathed beaks." Queequeg represents what Charles Olson, in his ground-breaking 1947 study of *Moby-Dick,* calls "Pacific Man," a way of living in intimate contact with the more-than-human sea. In this way of life neither sharks nor sea-hawks threaten, and the sea itself echoes the "dirge" in a mourning survivor's soul. Ishmael doesn't go mad, like Pip, during his solitary swim. But that's because he clings to a coffin that surfaces out of a deep fantasy about the interpenetration of humankind and the ocean.

Egeon's Rescue

"I think you all have drunk of Circe's cup" (5.1.271), says the Duke as the misidentifications of *The Comedy of Errors* reach climax. This line culminates the transformative and Odyssean subtexts of the play. It's hard to know how well Shakespeare knew Homer's work, and it's possible that he relied only on second-hand evidence through Virgil, Ovid, and others, but in these traditions Circe represents both a figure for bestial transfiguration and a goddess of the sea. (Spenser's Acrasia, another Circe-figure, also emphasizes her maritime connections; getting to her Bower requires Odyssean navigation.) Shakespeare's audience has been well-prepared for the untangling of identities that comes when Egeon, Emilia, and the two sets of twins finally appear on stage at the same time. The Duke's line emphasizes that unsnarling the plot requires countering the ocean's black magic. The play's narrative instability, born of shipwreck and immersion, derives from the sea on literal and metaphorical levels. Egeon recovers his family by performing, over a generation, a maritime rescue operation like Queequeg's.

Egeon's last lines reprise his survival story, as the sight of his lost wife wrenches him back to the long-ago catastrophe. "If I dream not," he says, "thou art Emilia; / If thou art she, tell me, where is that son / That floated with thee on the fatal raft?" (5.1.352–4). Egeon has fallen back into deep water, but rather than being stuck in a "heartless immensity" like Pip, he retrospectively unifies his family on the "fatal" (which now proves merciful) raft. Rather than drowning like Queequeg, Egeon survives, but more through reassembling his patchwork human community than through engaging directly with the waters. His final word, "raft," emphasizes that he's not really a swimmer; he (like Ishmael) needs help to stay afloat.

As the first of a series of Mediterranean plays that includes *The Merchant of Venice*, *Twelfth Night*, *Othello*, *Antony and Cleopatra*, *Pericles*, and *The Tempest*, *The Comedy of Errors* frames this sea as problematic but survivable. What the Pacific was for Melville, the Med was for Shakespeare: the sea as ideal literary subject. Ishmael insists that for "any meditative Magian rover, this serene Pacific . . . must . . . be the sea of his adoption" because of sheer size and exoticism: "this mysterious, divine Pacific zones the world's wide bulk about; makes all coasts one bay to it; seems the tide-beating heart of the earth" (367). Had Shakespeare been more attuned to the ways the Atlantic would change English (and world) history, he might have focused his attention there, but the eastern Mediterranean, with its classical history, biblical geography, and Turkish imperial culture, was Shakespeare's favorite literary ocean. Egeon's shipwreck floats before the other maritime plays like a proleptic threat, a catastrophic fate that strikes Viola and Pericles and colors the voyages of Antony and Othello. Surviving immersion takes time, patience, and luck, and it helps to be in a play that trumpets its genre in its title. But Egeon, whose story is more Odyssean homecoming or Greek romance than comedy, finds loss and mystery in the waters more than treasure or wisdom. He doesn't show the combativeness of Ferdinand or the natural grace of Queequeg or even Trinculo, but instead encounters the deeply unsettling knowledge that being in water, rather than on land, produces.

Chapter 4
Beachcombing: *Twelfth Night*

We who are born of the ocean can never seek solace
in rivers: their flowing runs on like our longing,
reproves us our lack of endeavor and purpose,
proves that our striving will founder on that.
(Kamau Brathwaite, "The South")

The ocean changes people. Literary depictions of the purifying powers of the sea are at least as old as Euripides, who wrote "The sea washes away and cleanses every human stain" in *Iphigenia at Tauris*. Baptism, usually with fresh water, became central to Christian theology but was already in place at Delphi. The idea that physical encounters with salt water have medicinal consequences, that a bit of sea-bathing is just what a body needs to set it up forever, peaked with the explosion of seaside tourism in eighteenth-century Europe. No one spoke more ecstatically about the impact of water on human bodies than Dr. Hughes Maret, whose study of the medicinal effects of fresh- and sea-water won first prize at the Academy of Bordeaux in 1766. Maret insisted that the benefits of the sea were spiritual as well as physical: when a person goes into the ocean, Maret claims, "a prodigious upheaval occurs through the whole body; the soul, surprised by such an expected event, startled by the fear of disunion from the body that it thinks is close at hand, lets the reins of government of the body over which it presides drop, so to speak." A temporary disjunction of the soul from the body, a splitting of the self when faced with the prospect of mortality, a reaction so deeply physical that it becomes spiritual: these were the consequences of ocean bathing one and one-half centuries after Shakespeare. In *Twelfth Night*, the ocean creates something like the same consequences, if not the same intensity. The play's central narrative, in which two bodies with "one face, one voice, one habit" (5.1.200) are thrown into the surf and "two persons" (5.1.200) emerge, provides a prehistory of Maret's understanding of the destabilizing force of salt water. The twins get reborn in stormy seas. On a metaphoric level, the turbulent water divides a unitary hermaphrodite into two bodies, female Viola and male Sebastian. These sundered forms then destabilize ale-soaked Illyria. Proximity to the sea creates possibility in this coastal drama. The ocean's capacity for rupture, disorder, and rebirth undergirds *Twelfth Night* in terms that parallel Maret's sea-cure. Joyce's Buck Mulligan feels the same visceral power in "the snotgreen sea, the scrotumtightening sea." Nothing like water to make a new you.

Like *The Comedy of Errors*, *Twelfth Night* explores a society saturated with ocean. Located in Illyria, an equally mystical, if less Christian, corner of the Turkish Mediterranean, the play begins when Viola and Sebastian escape from the sea into Orsino's and Olivia's emotional oceans. *Twelfth Night* envisions a hedonic, erotic, and self-indulgent beach culture that feels oddly modern. The seashore, cultural historians tell us, did not emerge as an object of fascination in European culture until eighteenth-century figures like Maret touted its benefits. (Some critics, including W. H. Auden, argue that the modern sea was born with Romanticism.) But Shakespeare's play, unlike Maret's patients, does not seek out the ocean so much as register its constant abiding presence. The play's embrace of the shore as part of its cultural landscape emerges most clearly alongside the works of modern Caribbean poets like Kamau Brathwaite and Derek Walcott. Both the play and these poets use poetry to connect human emotions to the ocean. In Brathwaite's "The South," for example, part of *The Arrivants* (1973), the disjunction between rivers, which he associates with cities like London and New York, and the warm oceans of Africa and the Caribbean maps the poet's distance from the imperial center. Like Viola, Brathwaite makes a reluctant traveler, "borne down the years . . . past pains that would wreck us, sorrows arrest us." But unlike Shakespeare's heroine, Brathwaite knows the sea. The wordless but deep knowledge that comes from being "born of ocean" creates a physical intimacy that precludes the radical shock of Maret's immersion. Caribbean poets like Brathwaite and Walcott offer this oceanic proximity to thalassological readings of Shakespeare. Viola's arc in the play moves her from Maret's shock to Brathwaite's knowledge. She learns to live with the sea.

On the Beach

Hands reached into water;
gods nudged us like fish;
black bottomless whales that we worshipped.
   (Kamau Brathwaite, "The White River")

What is the difference between Illyria and Elysium? What does being in the sea, that turbulent space Brathwaite calls a "White River," do to the twins? When Viola emerges from the ocean, her first concern is location: "What country, friends, is this?" (1.2.1). Her time in the surf has disoriented her so that she cannot recognize the coast that (presumably) her ship was near when it split. The answer, Illyria, combines two contexts: classical Greece and Ottoman Turkey. The name is ancient, derived from Illyrius, the son of Cadmus and Harmony. But the country was, in Shakespeare's lifetime, under Turkish control. Like Ephesus and the multiple cities of *Pericles*, it sits squarely within Shakespeare's exotic eastern Med. By contrasting Illyria with Elysium, land of the happy dead, Viola emphasizes that she hovers between life in a new land and death beneath the waves. Her language recalls the ancient maxim, which the minister John Flavell cites in *Navigation Spiritualiz'd* (1698), that mariners should not be numbered among either the living or the dead, but comprise "as it were, a Third sort of Persons . . . their Lives hanging continually in suspense before them." Like these sailors, Viola hangs between worlds. Her language also invokes the other "split" that the shipwreck created, between her twin and her self. Her body – the female half of the whole – washes up in Illyria. But Sebastian, her male half, remains at sea.

The sea works indirectly in this scene, and a performance need make no visible gesture toward the water itself. Unlike Egeon, Viola does not directly describe her sea-rebirth. The descriptive passage that most closely parallels Egeon's narrative, in fact, is the Captain's description of Sebastian. Viola's passivity introduces Sebastian's struggle, previewing a gendered joke about male power and female passivity the play will later indulge when Sebastian bloodies Sir Toby's coxcomb (5.1.165–7). But Sebastian's swimming, while active, lacks the martial, combative language of Ferdinand in *the Tempest*. The captain describes a water-lover, not a fighter:

> I saw your brother,
> Most provident in peril, bind himself,
> Courage and hope both teaching him the practice,
> To a strong mast that lived upon the sea;
> Where, like Arion on the dolphin's back,
> I saw him hold acquaintance with the waves
> So long as I can see.

$$(1.2.11–17)$$

Fittingly in a play that draws heavily on Greek romance, Sebastian's combat with the waters is "provident," not violent. By "bind[ing] himself" to the "strong mast," Sebastian limits his mobility and relies on the remains of the ship. (Lashing one's self to flotsam was a common tactic in rough waters, but it also amounts to assuming a passive stance. Egeon and Emilia tie themselves to their mast, but more active figures such as Ferdinand, and Robinson Crusoe, swim to shore.) To "hold acquaintance with the waves" brings Sebastian into the direct contact with the salt water that would change Egeon's life and the lives of Maret's patients. The striking image of the mast that "lived upon the sea" anticipates Sebastian's sexual potency, and also gestures toward the aquaman fantasy of a human life amid the waters. Later references to Sebastian being pulled out of a "breach of the sea" (2.1.5) and his "flood of fortune" (4.3.11) when he meets Olivia activate the sexual pun in "acquaintance" that also appears in Malvolio's reading of "her c's, her u's, and her t's" (2.5.71–2). Caught between phallic mast and vaginal sea, Sebastian's passive and pleasurable struggle contrasts sharply with Ferdinand's epic combat. The watery Elysium from which the loving pirate Antonio rescues Sebastian combines provident and erotic acquaintance, masculine and feminine metaphors. The two twins, even after the waters separate them, mix their genders and social functions.

Viola's beachy mixture of male and female qualities emerges from her isolation; first she gets separated from the sea and her brother, and later from Illyrian society. Throughout the play, she is a woman apart, not addressed by her own name until she is reunited with Sebastian the last scene. (He is the first to speak her name, 5.1.226.) Even what appears to be a fossil plot-element, her initial desire to present herself to Orsino "as an eunuch" (1.2.56), speaks to her exclusion from the overtly sexualized culture of the Duke's court (as well as underlining Illyria's Turkishness). Viola understands herself as trapped in passivity, "like Patience on a monument" (2.4.111), imprisoned within her page-boy disguise. She hides in the guise of Cesario as the waves hide her before the first scene; both conceal her inside an identity she cannot claim. Unlike the cross-dressed connivers Portia and Rosalind, Viola does little to advance her cause; she simply hopes that "tempests are kind, and salt waves fresh in love" (3.4.324). The two halves of this line inscribe the limits of her power. The first half places her, like Ferdinand, Pericles, or Jonah, at the mercy of the tempest, in the appropriate place for a romance heroine. The second half, however, asks for a change of venue, in which love remakes the ocean's salt as drinkable "fresh" water. Viola is not, however, in a fresh-water landscape like the Forest of Arden. She wanders a salty shore, on which it's helpful to plead with the storm but unwise to expect sympathy.

Viola understands the foreign element in which she finds herself to be time itself. In her longest soliloquy, she concludes, "O Time, thou must untangle this, not I; / It is too hard a knot for me t'untie" (2.2.35–6). Alongside her reference to "tempests," her invocation of "time" accents these two words' shared etymology, both deriving from the Latin *tempus*. (The French homology between time and the weather, both *temps*, makes the connection between duration and physical experience even more explicit.) Viola survives in time as in a stormy ocean, hanging on to "our driving boat" (1.2.11) while her twin struggles in the surf. Unlike Sebastian-as-Arion, Viola does not commune with her oceanic world. She holds herself apart from it.

A Prehistory of the Beach

> *Here at last was the rager,*
> *the growler, wet breather,*
> *life giver, white curly smoker*
> > *(Kamau Brathwaite, "The White River")*

The privileged cultural location for the separation and liminality that Viola represents is the place she begins the play, the beach. The no-man's-land of the seashore characterizes this play's classical-and-Turkish Illyria, its swirling mix of sentimentality, cynicism, and ale-soaked mirth. More than any of Shakespeare's maritime plays, *Twelfth Night* feels almost Caribbean: its waters are warm, translucent, sympathetic. Like Brathwaite in "The White River," Viola confronts the sea as both "rager" and "life giver." For Caribbean poets like Brathwaite and Walcott, the beach isn't marginal. It's the sandy face of the world, the place in which a body finds itself "at last." Viola's attempted self-discovery (and eventual recovery of her twin) takes place under the sign of the strand.

Cultural historians tell us that the modern craze for the seashore was "invented" in the eighteenth century. The burgeoning Grand Tour brought generations of English gentlemen to seaside towns like Sheveningen in Holland and the Virgil-haunted Bay of Naples, where classical education and emergent "natural theology" made them receptive to the charms of the ocean. But even if the "discovery of the seaside" in the European imagination occurred, as Alain Corbin has shown, between 1750 and 1840, its seeds germinated earlier. The expansion in maritime travel that began with the Portuguese exploration of the Canaries, Madeira, and the Azores in the fifteenth century, and in England a century later with the voyages of Raleigh, Drake, Cavendish, and others, generated a surge of interest in the maritime world, including (in England) the massive compilations of Hakluyt and Purchas. Artistic representations of the beach began to appear in paintings, emblems, and literary works such as Spenser's *Amoretti* 75 ("One day I wrote her name upon the strand"), Margaret Cavendish's "The Sea-Goddess," and in European poetry by Sannazaro, Luis Vaz de Camões, and Saint Amant (all influenced by the seaside topos in Virgil's *Georgics*). Plays like *Twelfth Night* reveal a nascent poetics of beachcombing that would emerge into mainstream English culture in the next century. The beach, a foreign no-place that resists human cultivation, represents what Jean-Didier Urbain calls the "aesthetics of the void." Wandering the strand with disconsolate Viola, we recognize how little it takes to unmoor us from the world.

Already in Shakespeare the beach represents what Corbin would later term a "focal point for the world's enigmas." The pleasures of ocean-watching would shift from the philosophical schadenfruede of Lucretius, in which the solidity of the shore emphasizes the insta-bility of the water, to something sublime and transformative. While sublimity as such would become a mainstream preoccupation only in the eighteenth century, Longinus's Greek treatise "On the Sublime," which would greatly influence Addison, Burke, Kant, and other Enlightenment theorists, was first published in Basel in 1554. Addison's claim in the *Spectator* that no object "affects my Imagination so much as the Sea or Ocean" (1712) emerges out of early eighteenth-century culture, but it also draws on earlier poetic representations of the sea, particularly Psalm 107 but arguably also Shakespeare's plays. Once writers crossed with Urbain calls the "frontier of the breaker," their view of the ocean was forever altered.

The beach as seventeenth-century artists represented it and eighteenth-century theorists understood it was a critical space, anti-pastoral, antirational, and antihuman. It contrasts sharply with early modern poetry's more widely known vision of the natural world, the garden. Even radical versions of the garden, including Marvell's and Milton's, are to some extent human-shaped. Eden, of course, is literally built for (a happier version of) humanity, but Marvel's "green thought / In a green shade" imagines nature interacting directly, if mysteriously, with the poet's imagination. The strand, by contrast, is disorderly and mutable; it exceeds any human rational order. According to the theory of the sublime, it is precisely this "outrage of the imagination" (Kant) that gives pleasure. For early modern artists like Shakespeare, who could not yet rely on theorists like Addison, Burke, and Kant, the disorder of sublimity challenged humankind's sense of itself in nature. Does the beach lead to Illyria, through the mingled heritage of Greek and Ottoman cultures, or to Elysium, the land of the dead? What would it take to find out?

The Sentimental Sea

Half my friends are dead . . .

Tonight I can snatch their talk
from the faint surf's drone
through the canes, but I cannot walk

on the moonlit leaves of ocean
down that white road alone
> *(Derek Walcott, "Sea Canes")*

Derek Walcott's poetry, especially lyric meditations like "Sea Canes" and the well-known "The Sea is History," present a sustained attempt to integrate the waters of the Caribbean into an artistic and cultural self-representation. The sea talks to Walcott, and he creates himself as a poet by talking back. The part of his poetic ocean that seems most relevant to *Twelfth Night* is his deep, salt-drenched emotionalism; for Walcott, as for Viola, the surf speaks to lost human connections, but it substitutes for them a blank, uninterpretable noise. What Walcott calls "the faint surf's drone" hints at but does not reveal the ocean's "white road" of death. "Moonlit leaves of ocean" speak to the poet as sentimental music speaks to Orsino; both are "food of love" (1.1.1), and both have "a dying fall" (1.1.4). Orsino makes the relationship between the sea and human emotions explicit:

> O spirit of love, how quick and fresh art thou,
> That, notwithstanding thy capacity
> Receiveth as the sea, naught enters there
> Of what validity and pitch soe'er,
> But falls into abatement and low price
> Even in a minute!

(1.1.9–14)

The slight confusion in Orsino's metaphors, between fresh and salt water, and between the sea's "abatement" and his own supposedly limitless love, unfolds the play's critique of his love-besotted ways. His self-contradictory attitude toward his own emotions – he asks music to overfeed his love so that "appetite may sicken and die" (1.1.3) – makes the sea a curious choice of metaphor: it functions both as a massive reservoir of emotional intensity, which the storm recapitulates in the next scene, and also as a fundamentally imperturbable thing, unchanged by additions or abatements. Orsino, like Walcott, sees himself in a sentimental sea, but unable to "snatch" the sea's "talk" like the modern poet, the Duke imagines himself lost in a vast ocean.

In the emotional hothouse of Illyria, the sea almost always seems a threat. Orsino emphasizes the ocean's destructive power when he tells the disguised Viola that his love is "all as hungry as the sea, / And can digest as much" (2.4.97–8). The dramatic irony that Orsino uses this metaphor to exaggerate the emotional force of male love to the loving female Viola emphasizes how little he understands himself when he invokes the sea. Orsino's traditional sense of the "hungry" ocean also colors the play's first description of Olivia, when she has sequestered herself, "water[ing] once a day her chamber round / With eye-offending brine" (1.1.28–9). For these melodramatic aristocrats, whose eventual marriages to the two twins underline their basic compatibility, salt water overwhelms human bodies; it proves too large to understand or resist. Even Orsino's final thankfulness that the sea has thrown up spouses for himself and Olivia gets described as an unexplained mystery: "I shall have share," he says, "in this most happy wreck" (5.1.251). Inverting his claim in the opening scene that his love will sink into the infinite sea, his gratitude for the delivery of the twins does little to reduce the foreign-ness of the ocean. Instead of taking untraceably, the waters now give, mysteriously.

The play's subplots also invoke water, but they treat its disorienting force as an invitation, not a threat. Feste declares, "I am for all waters" (4.2.47) as he toggles between playing Sir Topas and playing himself, and the quip underlines his shape-shifting omniverousness. (Notably, he and Viola are the only characters welcome in both Orsino's and Olivia's courts.) His play-closing song, which the Fool would reprise in *King Lear*, emphasizes the leveling and uniting power of water:

> A great while ago the world begun,
> With hey, ho, the wind and the rain
> But that's all one, our play is done,
> And we'll strive to please you every day.
> (5.1.382–5)

Feste's sympathy with water emphasizes that even comic standards like Sir Toby's bottomless thirst connect theatrical festivity to liquidity. Toby may be counseled to "leave drinking" (1.5.23), as Feste implies he should before marrying Maria, but the play insists that drinking produces a deeper understanding of human nature. "Dost thou think," Sir Toby asks Malvolio, "because thou art virtuous, there shall be no more cakes and ale?" (2.3.95–6). In the sea-suffused world of Illyria, ale and other liquids (Toby mentions "aqua vitae," 3.1.159) always flow, and the task is to come to terms with, not refuse, them.

The shipwrecked twins' experiences of the ocean are the play's deepest, and each notably receives the assistance of a maritime figure. The captain who rescues Viola in the ship's boat cuts a fairly traditional figure: a trusty mariner, with "fair behavior" and "a mind that suits / With this thy fair and outward character" (1.2.47, 50–1). Sebastian's rescuer, however, who must work harder to "redeem" his charge from "the rude sea's enraged and foamy mouth" (5.1.66–7), is, at least according to Orsino, "a notorious pirate" and "saltwater thief" (5.1.39). These two iconic opposites – the captain and the pirate, a lawful and lawless sailor – frame the twins' emergence from ocean to beach. Each salty helper accompanies his charge to Illyria, in Antonio's case at great personal risk. The captain, who does not appear after the first act (though his testimony is appealed to in 5.1), represents an orderly, circumspect nautical world, and he helps Viola disguise herself in Orsino's court. Antonio, whose past includes "sea-fights[s] 'gainst the Count his galleys" (3.3.26) and who seems known by his "sea-cap" (3.4.271), represents the rougher seas of unconditional (and unrequited) love. When Viola denies Antonio, he describes his love for Sebastian in religious terms: "And to his image, which methought did promise / Most venerable worth, did I devotion" (3.4.303–4). Iconoclastic Protestants in the audience may have been put off by Antonio's idolatry, but attentive playgoers would have been reminded of Viola's love for Orsino. Like the twin who fails to recognize him, and like Walcott mourning lost friends, Antonio swims in seas he cannot understand.

Viola's Not

> *There's a fresh light follows a storm*
> *while the whole sea still havoc; in its bright wake*
> *I saw the veiled face of Maria Concepcion*
> *marrying the ocean . . .*
> (*Derek Walcott*, "*The Schooner* Flight")

At the heart of *Twelfth Night* Viola combs the Illyrian beach, searching first for her lost twin and later for a temporarily unattainable love. She resembles the thing she looks at. Like Iago, a more nefarious salty deceiver, she defines herself by denying her identity. "I am not what I am" (3.1.122), she tells Olivia, in words that anticipate Iago's. Viola's "not," her self-negation and radical distance from herself, underlie her beachcomber's identity. She's not the play's only deceiver – Malvolio, Maria, Toby, and Feste all disguise themselves – but she's the one who understands unstable identity as a problem. Unlike Iago, who exploits the power of negation, Viola struggles under the weight of her oceanic "not." To be "not what I am" opens her up to deeper fluctuations of selfhood than comic figures like Feste or even Malvolio endure. The destabilizing force of the seashore, the place in which she can't tell Illyria from Elysium, undergirds Viola's crisis of identity. She does not take Iago's path, which leverages maritime instability for destructive agency. Instead, she builds a contingent, flexible identity that seldom knows what it really is.

Her opening exchange with the captain emphasizes the contingency of seaside life. After she suggests that Sebastian may have survived – "Perchance he is not drowned" (1.2.5) – the captain reminds her of her own dependence on random chance: "It is perchance that you yourself were saved" (1.2.6). Viola's liminal, sea-borne self depends, fundamentally, on chance, and chance, as Ulrich Kinzel has shown, had become by the sixteenth century a symbolic feature of the sea. The shock of losing her twin leaves Viola without a clear purpose ("What should I do in Illyria?") and without a comprehensible narrative of her survival ("It is perchance . . ."). Like the "prodigious upheaval" that Maret imputes to sea-bathing, Viola's immersion empties her world and replaces it with nothingness. Her featureless strand and her "not" subtend the coded history she narrates to Orsino, in which she calls her supposed sister, "A blank, my lord" (2.4.107). Becoming a blank through never-revealed love returns Viola to the ever-opaque beach, but she brings with her an erotic charge. Blanks are also targets; Olivia later asks that Orsino's love-thoughts be "blanks, rather than filled with me" (3.1.86). To be a "blank," and a "not," only surviving "perchance," means existing on the margin of human society, largely excluded from the joys and jokes of court life. The comedy of *Twelfth Night* brings Viola back from this margin to the center of society, as she finally becomes her "master's mistress" and Olivia's "sister" (5.1.304). Faced with such largess, she does not speak in the play's last one hundred twenty-three lines. Unlike Walcott's hero Shabine, who sees his love "Maria Concepcion / marrying the ocean" after he survives a storm, Viola returns to the stable world of the land. In this play, at least, you can return from the sea.

What the Pirates Said to Hamlet

When you come back, set yourself down naked. Show your body, dripping wet. Let everyone see. That way you can keep your secrets.

Hungry ghosts will circle around you. Courtiers, soldiers, scholars. Brave new worlds of want. Also women.

Remember: we are men and women both. Created together. One trouser leg at a time.

We know what you should to do next. The waters have taught us, and their never-surfeited songs. We sail back and forth across the waves like wolves. England, Denmark, Norway – nutshells, all. Two-thirds of this terraqueous globe are ours.

Who doesn't love pirates? What is it about us: our beards, our blades, our tongues? The way we put girdles round about globes? When was it that you first wanted to sail away?

To be a sparrow does not become a king.

When the waters open before you like routes to undiscovered coast-lines, when the friends of your heart's core cannot play your stops, when girls take to nunneries and uncles to thrones – we know what you should do. We stopped our mothers' mouths long ago.

Pirates kill people, prince. That's why we are kings on the sea.

What is the pirate utopia but a place for play and murder? Where we kill for gain and pleasure? To be, temporarily, alone and autonomous, free as the sea, owing subscription to nor man nor beast? You feel it, and we know it – that place where seeming is more than being, where shows never stop, where music is less about order than power. The other side of the whale's road.

Sing it with us: Farewell and adieu, all ye Danish ladies . . .

Nothing's rotten in Denmark that a little blood won't wash clean. You know what your job is.

Make the green one red.

Chapter 5
Fishing: *Pericles*

Freckled whelp	One grand hooded phantom
Hag-born	A snow hill in the air
Slave	Dumb thing
Villain	Dismemberer
Earth	Demogorgon
Tortoise	Ubiquitous
Filth	Immortal
Hag-seed	Unexampled, intelligent malignity
Malice	Our one only and all-engrossing object
Fish	Job's whale
Indian	Brute
Devil	Whiteness
Monster	Indefiniteness
Cat	Albino
Mooncalf	Shaker God
Servant monster	Venerable moss-bearded Daniel Boone
Man-monster	Accursed thing
Deboshed fish	Glorified
Half a fish and half a monster	Grand old god
Beast	White living spot
Varlet	Fatal goal
Born devil	Glacier
Foot-licker	Murderous fish

Bully monster	Predestinating head
Plain fish	All-destroying but unconquering
Demi-devil	
Thing of darkness	

Caliban and Moby-Dick are the two biggest fish in the sea. They sprawl across our literary culture like odd-shaped colossi, alluring, disturbing, and always just out of reach. Melville's totemic whale, probably Anglophone literature's most vivid representation of the secrets of the deep, represents the explicitly supernatural (Demogorgon, Shaker God) at the heart of the sea. The White Whale's defining characteristic, however, is less divinity than opacity – or perhaps his divinity consists precisely of opacity. His whiteness is indefiniteness is ubiquitousness, always both dumb and predestinating. "Hast seen the White Whale?" goes Ahab's refrain, reminding all who cross his path that this God hides himself in the ocean. The whale never speaks, and neither Ahab's rage nor Ishmael's encyclopedic, insatiable curiosity captures him. Moby-Dick is like the sea: we see him but never comprehend him.

Caliban, by contrast, is the fish that never gets away. As Prospero says, "we cannot miss him," because he provides "offices / That profit us" (2.1.312–14). Unlike Moby-Dick, however, Caliban is not solely a watery creature. The "deboshed fish" smells like the ocean, but he is also "earth" and a "tortoise," not to mention "a born devil, on whose nature / Nurture can never stick" (4.1.188–9). As a hybrid, "half a fish and half a monster," and also a domesticable slave whom Prospero in the end can "acknowledge mine" (5.1.276), Caliban represents commodifiable value extracted from the maritime world. He's a good fish to catch, as sea-travelers from Prospero to Stephano discover. (Moby-Dick, by contrast, belongs to no one because he never gets caught.) Both Melville and Shakespeare emphasize that their sea-monsters are prizes for fisherman: they are valuable, exotic, and "no doubt marketable" (5.1.266). These two maritime creatures, semi-fish both, represent in their different ways what fishermen go down to the sea in ships to bring home: the whale oil that fueled the lamps of the nineteenth-century world, and the slave labor that built early modern Europe's global empires. Taking these fish out of the water – what Prospero manages but Ahab fails to do – means converting the ocean into portable property.

Through their resonant figurations of these prize fish, Melville and Shakespeare, in their different ways, show what drove English-speaking sailors to navigate the globe. As fish, Caliban and Moby-Dick elicit proto-imperial desire. Reading these two figures' epithets in parallel highlights their shared supernatural ancestry – Caliban is a "devil," Moby-Dick a "God" – and their threatening nature: Caliban is "malice," Moby-Dick "malignity" itself. As a semi-human linked organically and symbolically to "earth," Caliban threatens human bodies more intimately than his counterpart – it's hard to imagine any circumstance that would "people" the world with Moby-Dicks – but the vast potency of the White Whale (and the pun in his name) also contains a sexual threat. These two impossible commodities represent the wealth that comes out of oceans. They also exemplify ways of being in the sea that are beyond the reach of ordinary human experience. Even Queequeg cannot live in oceanic nature like Caliban or the white whale. To swim with these monsters is to be a body wholly body, fully and unbearably present in the physical world. Caliban, born on the magic island, hears its "sounds and sweet airs" (3.3.136) and knows its watery landscape, from the "best springs" to the mysterious "scamels from the rock" (2.2.157, 169). Moby-Dick dwells in fathomless depths from which only Jonah has returned. These two fish – one half a monster, the other a malignant God – represent the fantasy of a life that interacts more directly with primeval nature than human bodies can bear.

Shakespeare's most thorough investigation of fishing – understood broadly as the project of extracting value from the sea – does not appear in the fish-slave, or even in *The Tempest*'s reframing of imperial expansion through the exogamous over-plot of Claribel's marriage. Instead, fishing-for-empire appears most clearly in an earlier sea-play,

Pericles, in which the hero learns philosophy from fishermen, and his daughter emerges from the deep. In reading *Pericles* as fish-story, I suggest that this play anticipates Melville's sense of the boundless intensity of the ocean. To do this, I'll frame my reading of the play through *Moby-Dick*'s distinction between Fast- and Loose-Fish.

> *A Fast-Fish belongs to the party fast to it . . . A Loose-Fish is fair game for anybody who can soonest catch it.*
>
> (Moby-Dick)

Several years before *The Tempest* (1611), the oceans shifted from the margins to the center of Shakespeare's plays. Starting with *Pericles* (1607–8), the late romances foreground seafaring and the ocean. Shipwrecks appear in *Pericles, The Tempest, The Winter's Tale*, and (figuratively) in *Two Noble Kinsmen*, and even *Cymbeline* contains several sea journeys and scenes at Milford Haven. The shift toward the maritime contributes to the valedictory nature of this moment in Shakespeare's career; in turning back to the sea he reprises the dilemmas of Egeon and Viola and Iago. But salt water flavors the late plays more sharply than it had even *Othello*, and Melville's (partly fanciful) distinction between a Fast-Fist and a Loose-Fish helps explain why. Early and mid-career maritime figures like Othello and Viola strive to resist oceanic disorientation and stay Fast-Fish, while in the romances characters like Marina become radically Loose. (Ariel's and Caliban's twin struggles for freedom show two Fast-Fish trying, one successfully, to Loosen themselves.) The dramatic universe of Fast-Fish is a world of connections formed, broken, and renegotiated; it includes the stable narrative structures of dynastic history and erotic comedy, and it drives Egeon's and Viola's efforts to reunite families parted by the seas. Even Othello's doomed effort to fashion what Ahab calls "a personality . . . in the midst of the personified impersonal" attempts to keep Fast a suddenly Loosened life. Pericles's own story extends these struggles for stability amid erotic and political disruption; as travailing hero, the prince of Tyre's adventures parallel

protagonists from Hal to Hamlet. But the two-generation plot of
Pericles also takes up the Loose-Fish of Marina, whose connections
to family, nurse, foster-family, and even the counter-family of the
brothel get ruptured at every turn. She, as much as any figure in
Shakespeare's plays, represents what Queequeg was for Melville:
a thoroughly maritime human. Marina is Shakespeare's aquaman.
As this play shows, Shakespeare's depictions of sea-infused humanity
grow progressively darker and more Loose over the course of his
career: stoic Egeon begets empathetic Viola, who spawns nihilistic
Iago, who begets two supernatural offspring, more-than-human
Marina and semi-human Caliban. Drawing on legends of mermaids
and kelpies, Marina emerges from the depths into human society, but
her actions never lose the bitter tang of salt. Her solitary life and rise
to fortune demonstrate the power of coming to terms with the sea.
Her example suggests that living in an oceanic world may be possible,
but also that the usual supports of human culture, from family to
nation, provide little help.

Laws of the Sea

*These two laws touching Fast-Fish and Loose-Fish, I say, will, upon
reflection, be found the fundamentals of all human jurisprudence.*

(Moby-Dick)

During the early modern period, the sea's ancient status as alien God-
space was rearticulated so that it also became a symbol of freedom.
Once the Atlantic was crossed, and brave new worlds found in the
Americas and around Cape Horn and the Cape of Good Hope, the
sea was no longer just forbidding and alien, but also transformative
and liberating. The laws of this new space soon came into question,
and the Treaty of Tordesillas in 1494 split the globe into a Spanish
West (including the Caribbean) and Portuguese East (including
African islands like the Cape Verdes and Madeira, as well as the

Indian Ocean and much of the Pacific). The exact dividing line was often disputed, especially in the Pacific, where the location of the spice-producing Moluccas in relationship to Spanish and Portuguese territories was much debated in the 1520s and 1530s. Late-coming Northern Europeans nations like the Dutch and English would further disrupt Iberian claims. Modern maritime law is generally held to have begun with Hugo Grotius's *Mare liberum* (1609), which attacked the Portuguese monopoly of the East Indies trade. Grotius's brief articulated in legal terms the increasingly powerful cultural fantasy of oceanic liberty, but his ocean of Loose-Fish did not go unchallenged. English jurist John Seldon's *Mare Clausum* (1635), among others, forcefully argued for legal Fast-ness. The early modern ocean both invited and resisted legal control. *Pericles* explores precisely this two-faced sea.

The play's division between father-stories and daughter-stories enacts early modern culture's split understanding of open and closed oceans. Pericles, like Elizabethan voyagers and classical heroes, struggles to maintain social and personal bonds in the face of sea-borne disruption. His responsibilities to larger human communities – as prince, knight, suitor, husband, father, and political ally – make him a repeatedly Fast-Fish. Unlike the narrative traditions of *The Odyssey* and Greek romance, however, *Pericles* insists that homecoming does not end the story. The voyage of sea-born Marina inverts her father's: rather than being a Fast-Fish whose bonds are loosened, Marina starts Loose, unconnected, and incessantly mobile. She does not fashion a law or a polis out of the shores on which she is cast because she remains colored by the ocean's chaos. It's not a comfortable way to live – "This world to me is as a lasting storm" (4.1.18), she laments – but Marina embodies a fully marine life more than any previous Shakespearean character. Her maritime lament recalls the seafarer of the Old English lyric, and also Ezra Pound's reimagining of Odysseus's departure from Circe's island, "heavy with weeping." Marina the Loose-Fish represents an extreme case; like Caliban and Moby-Dick she emerges from the sea and carries its disorientation in her. The utopian project of *Pericles* imagines the aqua-woman as a musician, and transforms her rough music into a family-uniting harmony. Unlike Melville, whose divine whale swims alone in the depths, Shakespeare's boundary cases get drawn back into social worlds at the end of his romances, either awkwardly (as Caliban enters Prospero's extended family) or triumphantly (as Marina sails off to rule in Tyre). Pericles and his daughter will not live together at the play's end – he rules with Thaisa in Pentapolis, she with Lysimachus in Tyre – but they have remade the Eastern Med as a world safe for Fast- and Loose-Fish.

Princes and Fishermen

What to that redoubted harpooner, John Bull, is poor Ireland, but a Fast-Fish?

(Moby-Dick)

Pericles is a colonizer. His dominant concerns appear writ large in the full title of his play: "Prince of Tyre." Recent scholarship has tended to look elsewhere for Shakespeare's investigations of nascent British imperialism – to Prospero's island or Henry V's wars of conquest – but Pericles's protracted travels comprise a series of attempts to expand his kingdom's sway. He seeks an alliance through marriage with powerful Antioch, cultivates Tarsus with gifts of corn, seals an alliance with Pentapolis through marriage, and then, when he needs help, returns to Tarsus to redeem his debt. His aimless wandering in the second half of the play responds to the loss of his kingdom as much as his wife and daughter – or perhaps, to put it slightly differently, for a figure like Pericles to go back to Tyre with neither spouse nor heir constitutes a dereliction of imperial duty. His concern from the start of the play is with his land's security. "[L]et your cares o'erlook / What shipping and what lading's in our haven" (1.2.47–8), he orders his assembled lords, when his encounter with Antioch might be expected to distract him. He values Helicanus above his other retainers because Helicanus speaks for the communal needs of Tyre. The advisor's suggestion to his prince – "Go travel for a while" (1.2.104) – convinces Pericles that by playing the part of the romance hero, he serves his city.

The model Pericles follows for extracting value for his kingdom through traveling, however, differs from the conquests of Prospero or Henry V. Pericles is more fisherman than conquistador: rather than asserting his rule through arms or magic, he commits himself to several kinds of "hazard" (1.1.5) – first the riddle-game, then sea-travel, then the tournament. His encounter with the fishermen on the shores of Pentapolis (which may be in Greece, as the First Fisherman says [2.1.63], or Greek-speaking North Africa, as in Ortelius's 1595 map) clarifies the symbolic shape of his journeys. Listening to the fishermen joke about "rich misers" who resemble whales (2.1.29), Pericles recognizes that they are constructing allegories: "How from the finny subject of the sea / These fishers tell the infirmities of men . . ." (2.1.47–8). He then imagines that fish live inside a "watery empire" (2.1.49), thus reinforcing his focus on territorial expansion. While he has "never practised" (2.1.66) fishing, he joins the "honest fishermen" (2.1.51) in their "honest mirth" (2.1.92), and they teach him to catch political fish. Fishing here represents a new way for Pericles to extract value from the water; rather than marrying the daughter of a tyrant or rescuing a starving city, the prince finds on the shores of Pentapolis a new model for deriving sustenance directly from the sea.

Pericles can use fishing to expand his colonial ventures because life in the water reflects life on land, as in the fishermen's most celebrated exchange. "Master," says the third fisherman, "I marvel how the fishes lives in the sea." "Why," says the first fisherman, "as men do a-land: the great ones eat up the little ones" (2.1.26–9). This allegorical dialogue invokes the ancient tradition of piscatorial eclogues, a minor classical poetic sub-genre that was reintroduced to early modern Europe by Jacopo Sannazaro in Italian and Phineas Fletcher in English.

The fishermen's symbolic sea, which indicts the rich and grasping to praise the honest labor of common men, insulates Pericles's imperial project from one strain of political critique by linking him to workers who criticize landlords. Like Henry V, Pericles appears the sort of conqueror who has the goodwill of common working men. But the allegorizing process that the fishermen unleash does not work simply. Rather, the animal that represents the storm – the porpoise – bears its meaning through its refusal of simple categories. Porpoises predict storms, the third fisherman says, because they are not fully of either sea or land: "They say they're half fish, half flesh. A plague on them, they ne'er come but I look to be washed" (2.1.24–6). That porpoises and other marine mammals predicted storms was an early modern commonplace (Humphrey Gilbert's drowning in the north Atlantic in 1584 was prefigured by sighting a "lion of the Ocean sea"), but Shakespeare's elaboration of this topos suggests that the porpoise calls up the storm because it spans definitional categories. "Half fish, half flesh": the porpoise's bivalency threatens the fishermen's ability to keep sea and land separate. For characters who aspire to be Fast-Fish, like Pericles and the subjects of good King Simonides, the porpoise's hybridity unsettles their fixed categories.

Rather than hunting porpoises or whales, however, these fishermen salvage Pericles's royal and humanist identity – the identity that makes him a successful colonizer – by recovering his father's armor. They fish for Pericles's nobility. The prince, upon seeing the armor, emphasizes that it reconnects him to his "heritage, / Which my dead father did bequeath to me" (2.1.119–20). He further suggests that this salvaged treasure will enable him to extend his father's legacy: "My shipwrack now's no ill, / Since I have here my father gave in his will" (2.1.129–30). The armor that the fishermen rescue from the sea enables Pericles to join the tournament and win a royal bride in Pentapolis. The fishermen repeatedly emphasize the knight's dependence on their maritime labor. As they draw in the net, the second fisherman inserts the armor into the now-familiar allegory of rich against poor: "Here's a fish hangs in the net like a poor man's right in the law; 'twill hardly come out" (2.1.112–14). The same fisherman later jokes that the Prince owes the armor to him as much as to his royal father: "Ay, but hark you, my friend, 'twas we that made up this garment through the rough seams of the waters" (2.1.145–6). The sea/seams pun emphasizes that the armor (and with it Pericles's identity) returned to him through the rage of the sea-storm, and further, perhaps, that the raging waters are now part of Pericles's combat gear. Briefly recalling Mark Antony ("Now like a man of steel," 4.4.33), Pericles strides toward Pentapolis as an imperial warrior: "I am clothed in steel, / And spite of all the rapture of the sea / This jewel holds his binding on my arm" (2.1.150–2). Reconstituted by the fishermen (from whose labor he requests a "pair of bases," 2.1.157), Pericles reenters the world of Fast-Fish with his family jewel on his arm. He has seen the sign of the porpoise, but escaped.

Born at Sea

> *What are all men's minds and opinions but Loose-Fish?*
> (Moby-Dick)

Marina's relationship with the sea is more visceral; she first appears wet and never really dries off. Born at sea and later described by Dionyza as "Thetis' birth-child" (4.4.41), Marina represents the most sea-drenched character in all of Shakespeare's plays. She eclipses the expertise of sailors like the Boatswain, who labor at sea but remain creatures of the land, and approaches the marine animality of Caliban. (Her father, by contrast, is a skilled mariner; Marina describes him "haling ropes," 4.1.53.) Neither sailor nor fish, Marina is nonetheless nearer home at sea than anywhere else. Her birth occurs off-stage, presumably during Pericles' rant against the storm (3.1.1–14), and when she appears in Lychorida's arms the play shifts radically. The two-author schema that has become accepted wisdom about this play – that George Wilkins wrote (most of) the first two acts, and Shakespeare (most of) the last three – helps explain the shift in tone when the sea-born babe arrives. Attribution studies are always problematic, however, and in *Pericles* as it exists now (in editions prepared to modern editorial standards) the changes at this moment juxtapose Pericles's colonial ethic – his desire to expand his empire – against Marina's ocean-born Loose-ness. Even as a newborn, she fractures unitary meanings. She gets introduced as "this piece / Of your dead queen" (3.1.17–18), and Pericles recognizes that the world as she experiences it does not cohere:

> For a more blusterous birth had never babe . . .
> Thou hast as chiding a nativity
> As fire, air, water, earth and heaven can make
> To herald thee from the womb.
> Even at the first thy loss is more than can
> Thy portage quit.
>
> (3.1.21, 32–6)

While the rare word "portage" has caused editorial controversy, its dual connections to maritime cargo and to the Latin *portare*, to carry a child, suggests that Marina's birth ruptures both biological and nautical systems of delivery. Her name underscores her primary connection to sea, and her father even calls her "this fresh new seafarer" (3.1.41). When Pericles delivers the child to Cleon and Dionyza, his language implies an exchange, in which the sea takes Thaisa but the land receives Marina:

>   Could I rage and roar
> As doth the sea she [Thaisa] lies in, yet in the end
> Must be as 'tis. My gentle babe Marina,
> Whom for she was born at sea I have named so,
> Here I charge your charity withal.
>
> (3.3.10–14)

In the play's final acts, Marina becomes an object of exchange in the eastern Mediterranean, moving from Tarsus to Mytilene to Ephesus to Tyre. Her itinerary inverts her father's, as her unraveling of bonds counters his colonialist efforts to forge connections.

Rupture punctuates Marina's life, and at each turn disaster arrives by sea. Her birth comes during a storm; pirates, men of the sea, end her childhood; and her father's ship arrives at Mytilene by sea. The pirates, who here as in *Hamlet* serve as a narrative shorthand for radical disruption, deliver her from an African lion ("Leonine") back to the ocean. But already she has shown that the land is not her place: her first lines in the play – "No, I will rob Tellus of her weed" (4.1.12) – resist the goddess of earth. She describes herself, "Born in a tempest when my mother died" (4.1.17), as an alien creature, and her self-isolation at the "sea-margent" (4.1.25) enables Dionyza's treachery. Her exchange with Leonine suggests that the only story that matters to her is the story of her birth:

When I was born the wind was north . . .
Never was waves nor wind more violent,
And from the ladder tackle washes off
A canvas-climber.

(4.1.50, 58–60)

The sailor ("canvas-climber") washed into the sea anticipates the fate of Marina herself, torn from the rigging of her aristocratic foster-family. As a young woman, she remains inside her "lasting storm." Even in her birth-scene as she remembers (or reconstructs) it, her father's tactics of navigation and political control cannot help her. "The boatswain whistles," she explains, "and / The master calls and trebles their confusion" (4.1.62–3). In Marina's world, whistles and calls only increase disorder.

Marina's defining instability shows itself in moments of narrative transition, especially her birth and capture by pirates. A textually controversial piece of poetry, the epitaph that Dionyza displays on

Marina's monument, captures the heroine's spanning of the contested boundaries between land and sea. While the verse seems awkward even for Wilkins, to say nothing of Shakespeare, its central metaphor locates Marina in the flux between elements:

> She was of Tyrus the King's daughter
> On whom foul death hath made this slaughter.
> Marina was she called, and at her birth
> Thetis being proud swallowed some part o'th'earth.
> Therefore the earth, fearing to be o'erflowed,
> Hath Thetis' birth-child on the heavens bestowed;
> Wherefore she does, and swears she'll never stint,
> Make raging battery upon shores of flint.
>
> (4.4.36–43)

The metaphor is confused, with "part o'th' earth" seeming to represent both Thaisa and the headland on which the monument is placed. (The image perhaps recalls Camões's Adamastor, the Titan transformed into the rocky promontory of the Cape of Good Hope as punishment for his rebellion and lust after the sea-nymph Thetis [*Lusiads* 5.39–60].) The emphasis on strife between Thetis's sea and dry land seems clear; Marina, whose chastity will receive its own "raging battery" at the hands of the world, gets fixed at the place of maximum violence, the land–sea boundary. It becomes, like her, a place of contestation, with the sea "swallow[ing]" earth and the land "fearing to be o'erflowed." Wicked Dionyza recognizes that "absolute Marina" (4.0.31) embodies a fundamental confusion: does she belong to sea or land? The land-based memorial remains divided because so much of Marina remains in the water. Her birth at sea and (supposed) death on the beach tie her to the unending struggle of the roiling waters encroaching on the shore.

Marina's movement from ship to beach to city isolates her from her native element. Her relative distance from the water in urban Mytilene underlines the city's danger to her; it's a maritime city, but she appears neither on a boat nor on a beach. The brothel is the only setting in the play that removes her from direct proximity to the ocean. The storm and even the pirates are mobile and marine, Loose-Fish like Marina, but the inverted family-home of Bawd, Boult, and Pandar coops her up. The brothel attempts to turn Marina into a commodity, an exotic import who "would serve after a long voyage at sea" (4.5.40–1). The economy of the brothel refigures that of the fishermen: they show Pericles how to extract valuable items from the sea, while the brothel attempts to turn a sea-creature like Marina into one of a "dozen of virginities" (4.5.27–8). Taken away from her element, Marina resembles a beached whale; she temporarily loses mobility and power.

To recover in the land-locked brothel, Marina adopts the seaman-like tactics of Iago, converting Lysimachus through refusing to answer his questions. Unlike Iago, however, who fuels Othello's jealousy with carefully deployed negation, Marina manipulates Lysimachus through indirection. She deflects him without rejecting him; her responses – "What trade, sir?" "I cannot be offended with my trade" "E'er since I can remember" "Earlier too, sir, if now I be one" "Who is my principal?" (4.5.72, 74, 77, 81, 89) – never fully negate his questions. If Iago's "I am not that I am" nihilism recalls the ocean's refusal of any fixed shape, Marina's patient deflections follow the slow pattern of the surf eroding a stone. When she appeals directly to Lysimachus, she asks for freedom:

> O, that the gods
> Would set me free from this unhallowed place,
> Though they did change me to the meanest bird
> That flies in'th' purer air!
>
> (4.5.103–6)

She wants to be a bird, not a fish, but her plea for immersion in the "purer air" suggests that she craves the freedom of being an animal in nature. Like Caliban, she bridges the divide between human estrangement from the natural world and an animal's instinctive connection with it.

In escaping the brothel, however, Marina acts less as a part of nature than as skilled worker. She pays her way out of the brothel with aristocratic labor, telling Bolt: "If that thy master would make gain by me, / Proclaim that I can sing, weave, sew, and dance" (4.5.185–6). She learned these skills through the "princely training" (3.3.16) that Pericles asked Cleon and Dionyza to provide her in Tarsus. To some extent this episode simply flatters the upper class figures in Shakespeare's audience by emphasizing the practical value of an aristocratic education. Marina appears as a court lady who has learned her lessons well, and her musical accomplishments look backward to her parents' courtship in Pentapolis and forward to the music she plays for her father in act 5. But weaving and sewing also connect her to the civilized arts that the Greeks called *techne*, in which maritime skills feature prominently. In classical culture, the *techne* of the sea – sailing, navigation, boat-building, sail-making – represent the pinnacle of human skilled interaction with the natural world. Marina's arts are social and feminine, but her *metis* – her skill in making – connects her to Odysseus, the greatest tool-maker and mariner in the humanist pantheon. The heroine's Loose oceanic nature gets domesticated at the play's end by marriage and her assumption of royal power in Tyre. The arts she practices in Mytilene represent a way-station on her journey from the sea into civilization. Music, including the "rough and woeful music" (3.2.87) that Cerimon uses to wake Thaisa, serves in this play as the master-art that joins the death-world of the sea to the social spaces of land. Marina's musical and courtly education bridges this gap. But the sea still occupies the center of her play.

Two Storms

What is the great globe itself but a Loose-Fish?
(Moby-Dick)

The two sea-storms in *Pericles* provide slightly different visions of the sea's antihuman power, the first generating fatalistic passivity and the second proto-ecological intermingling. These set-pieces, full of tropes familiar to early modern humanists from Virgil, Ovid, Lucan, and Homer, temporarily rupture humankind's ability to survive the marine environment. The repetition of two nearly identical storms (2.1 and 3.1) facilitates the play's careful examination of the strife between sea and ship. The resonant narrative topos of a ship in storm, often featured in emblems and paintings, represents human efforts to survive in a hostile environment. The first storm suggests, traditionally enough, that shipwrecks show the hand of Fortune taking control of human events. The only proper response is fatalistic acceptance. The second storm, however, while repeating familiar tropes about hostile Fortune, suggests a more intimate interrelationship with the violent waters. During this storm, when Marina is born, Pericles intuits something of her deeper and more fundamental connection to the sea. The Fast-Fish, briefly, sees how it feels to be Loose.

The first storm, which wrecks Pericles off Pentapolis, resembles the "standard means of transportation" that, according to Northrop Frye, shipwrecks provide in Hellenistic romances. Like the princes in the *New Arcadia*, Pericles (whose name echoes Sidney's Pyrocles) must submit to Fortune – "All perishen of man, of pelf, / Ne aught escapend but himself" (2.0.35–6) – in order to wash up in the kingdom where he finds his destined wife. Gower's sing-song rhymes make this episode sound like a parody of humanist understandings of Fortuna: "Till Fortune, tired with doing bad, / Threw him ashore to give him glad" (2.0.37–8). Pericles' oration against the storm, despite its echoes of *King Lear*, emphasizes submission: "Yet cease your ire, you angry stars of heaven! / Wind, rain and thunder, remember earthly man / Is but a substance that must yield to you" (2.1.1–3). Pericles describes a straightforwardly hierarchical nature, in which the stars control the upper elements of wind, rain, and thunder, and "earthly man" waits on the bottom. These lines, generally assumed to be Wilkins's, drive home their meaning through Gower-like moralistic couplets: Pericles notes that the storm has left him of "breath / Nothing to think of but ensuing death" (2.1.6–7), and the speech ends with "watery grave" rhyming with "all he'll crave" (2.1.10–11). Unlike Lear's rant, and also unlike the active image of Pericles's seamanship that Marina later describes (4.1.51–5), this speech emphasizes passivity. Only after learning new kinds of activity from the fishermen and the tournament does Pericles learn to shift for himself.

Whether act 3 represents Shakespeare's authorial debut or not, the shift from submission to the distant stars in the first shipwreck to a more visceral appeal to the waters in the second marks a new way of engaging the marine world. Gower's introductory verse is again in four-beat couplets, and again invokes Fortuna's control, but now the goddess does not move simply; instead, "Fortune's mood / Varies" (3.0.46–7). Where act 2 had imagined a binary Fortune, making the hero's world either "bad" or "glad," now she creates variety. Even the ship's response to the second storm changes; it does not simply get dashed on the shore but sails wildly, "as a duck for life that dives" (3.0.49). Resembling the aquatic animal that Trinculo takes as his swimming model, Pericles's ship sails "up and down" (3.0.50), and while this vessel does not seem at home in the sea, it survives the storm. The dramaturgic shift from staging only the aftermath of the storm (Pericles enters 2.1 on shore) to making "[t]he stage the ship" (3.0.59) directs the play's attention more closely to the entanglement of human bodies with rough water.

The storm-soliloquy that opens 3.1 echoes its predecessor in act 2, but the shift from first speech's distant stars to the second's appeal to the god of the sea underlines a newly direct focus on the ocean. Pericles calls on Neptune as "[t]he god of this great vast" (3.1.1), indicating that he seeks a supernatural power in, not above, the water. The reference to Aeolus, "thou that hast / Upon the winds command" (3.1.2–3), echoes the language of Christ's disciplines on the Sea of Galilee (Luke 8:25), but by attributing this power to a pagan deity the play exchanges the abstractions of monotheism for a polytheistic world of natural spirits. (Nature, as Edmund emphasizes in *King Lear*, is pagan.) The storm's "surges / . . . wash both heaven and hell" (3.1.1–2), in the familiar metaphor, but the natural element that envelops the ship remains wholly uninterpretable. Seamanship fails to save the day: "[t]he seaman's whistle / Is as a whisper in the ears of death, / Unheard" (3.1.8–10). The connection that brings Pericles back to a human world, finally, is childbirth; his prayers shift to Lucina as Lychorida enters with the infant Marina. Her storm-tossed birth emerges under the sign of Fortune's variety and the water's violence. Pericles's symbolic task will be to salvage human order from the storm's flux. But he needs help from his disorderly daughter.

Marine Living

> *And what are you, reader, but a Loose-Fish and a Fast-Fish too?*
> (Moby-Dick)

The triumph of Marina the Aquawoman comes in the long recognition scene, in which her beauty, her "sweet harmony" (5.1.37), her life story, and finally her name draw her father (and herself) back into civilization. When Pericles finally recognizes his lost daughter, his attention suddenly shifts back to the sea. "O Helicanus," he cries in the beginning of his longest speech since act 3,

> strike me, honoured sir,
> Give me a gash, put me to present pain,
> Lest this great sea of joys rushing upon me
> O'erbear the shores of my mortality
> And drown me with their sweetness.
>
> (5.1.180–4)

Still a fisherman, Pericles imagines Marina as a lost treasure: "Thou that wast born at sea, buried at Tarsus, / And found at sea again!" (5.1.186–7). Only a final voyage to Ephesus to retrieve Thaisa remains before Pericles can fulfill his youthful ambition of an Eastern Mediterranean empire, with himself and Thaisa ruling in Pentapolis, closely allied with Marina and Lysimachus in Tyre. The irony that the Aquawoman's reward is a landed kingdom emphasizes how foreign her experience has been: what kind of kingdom would really suit her?

Marina, the enabling force behind Pericles's at-last successful colonial venture, remains Loose to the end, finally ruling a city she has never before seen. Her power, captured in her name, consists of a being-in-the-sea that no other human character in Shakespeare equals. Even Caliban, half-fish and unapt seducer, does not really match her watery charisma. With the possible exception of Cleopatra as "serpent of old Nile" (1.5.26), the heroine who most resembles Marina, albeit briefly, is drowned Ophelia, whose death occasions a brief but suggestive anticipation of Marina's water-infused nature. Gertrude describes Ophelia's clothes as resonant symbols of her doomed intimacy with water:

> Her clothes spread wide
> And mermaid-like awhile they bore her up,
> Which time she chanted snatches of old lauds
> As one incapable of her own distress,
> Or like a creature native and endued
> Unto that element.

$$(4.7.174-8)$$

Ophelia resembles a mermaid and appears almost native to the water, but Marina (nearly) embodies both. Laertes's mordant joke, "Too much of water hast thou, poor Ophelia" (4.7.183), registers the impossibility of human beings living deeply in the aquatic world. Marina's life-story, and her play, entertain a more hopeful, if still disorienting, version of this fantasy. But she remains, like the white whale and Queequeg, a Loose-Fish who can only partly be understood and never really caught. Her rule in Tyre seems likely to be as uncertain as her father's.

Chapter 6
Drowning: *Timon of Athens*

He swam the seas before the continents broke water; he once swam over the site of the Tuleries, and Windsor Castle, and the Kremlin. In Noah's flood he despised Noah's Ark; and if ever the world is again to be flooded, like the Netherlands, to kill off its rats, then the eternal whale will still survive, and rearing upon the top-most crest of the equatorial flood, spout his frothed defiance to the skies.

(Moby-Dick, "*Does the Whale's Magnitude Diminish?*")

What if the world hates us? What if drowning is the end toward which everything points? What if there is no dry spot left for human bodies in a world of salt? These are the final questions the sea poses in its immensity and hostility. Like Poor Tom in the storm, human bodies in the sea have no comfortable place to live. Once you're in, you have to get out. The threat of drowning colors all sea-stories as a constant danger and possible outcome. The heroism of mariners from Odysseus to Pericles, and swimmers from Egeon to Queequeg, comprise a series of delaying tactics, putting off the inevitable result of prolonged contact between water and the human body. The sea is not our home. If we stay too long, we drown.

The story of Western culture's responses to the sea begins with Greek bodies learning the difference between fresh water and salt. Narcissus's love for his reflection in a pool represents the sympathy between fresh water and humanity, while Odysseus's painful voyages underline the ocean's hostility. As Charles Sprawson has suggested, the modern West mixes three different water-cultures: the Greeks, who loved water; the Norse, who feared it; and the Romans, who built with it. Stories about immersion and survival function as narrative experiments, in which things from which humans seldom recover – shipwreck and drowning – represent limit-cases of living in an oceanic world. The legend of Aristotle's drowning, vociferously discounted by historians since the seventeenth century, shows the philosopher hurling himself into the sea because he was frustrated at not being able to explain the violent tidal shifts in the narrow channel between mainland Greece and the island of Euboea. To early modern Europe Aristotle typified reason and the intellectual qualities Western civilization values. The sea, in this story, represents everything in nature that will not yield up its secrets to philosophy. Aristotle's drowning inverts Lucretius's shipwreck with spectator paradigm: unable to bear watching something he cannot understand, Aristotle wrecks himself. The intellectual problem of the tides, which was not fully solved until Lord Kelvin's harmonic analysis in 1867, here represents the impossible goal of fully comprehending nature. Aristotle's mastery of the physical world stops at the shore, despite his invention of proto-sciences from meteorology to zoology. The moment when bodies enter salt water represents the absolute loss of human control.

Shakespeare stages the deathly seashore as the final resting place of Timon of Athens. Timon, seeking a home for his virulent misanthropy and rejection of the social world, places his body astride the boundary between the social world that has rejected him and the natural world in which he cannot live. "Come not to me again," he instructs his Steward,

> but say to Athens,
> Timon hath made his everlasting mansion
> Upon the beached verge of the salt flood,
> Who once a day with his embossed froth
> The turbulent surge shall cover.
>
> (5.1.213–7)

Timon's beach is a place of paradox, and the tension inside his epitaph (the first of four the play gives him) between his desire for an "everlasting mansion" and the ceaseless change and violence of the surf captures the play's vision of hostile nature. The world of "embossed froth" and "turbulent surge" exceeds human comprehension, like Aristotle's tides. When the waves "cover" Timon's body, they obscure his physical remains but also comprise a monument that is more "everlasting" than the statues (or poems) that function as memorials elsewhere in Shakespeare. *Timon of Athens*, like *Pericles* a joint-authored play (and, also like *Pericles*, an extension of *King Lear*'s radical antagonism toward nature), uses the sea to represent that part of the natural world into which humanity enters only in death. Expanding on the watery paths not taken by Egeon and Marina, Timon embraces the inhumanity of the ocean.

Aristotle

The tides of Euripus, the narrow strait between mainland Greece and the island of Euboea, were supposed by ancient observers to change direction seven times a day. These observers were misled by the violence of the tidal shifts; early modern observers began to discount the legend of Aristotle's death in part because they correctly concluded that these tides were regular, if dramatic. Thomas Browne, in *Psuedo-doxia Epidemica* (*Vulgar Errors*, 1672 [1646]), relates the then-familiar story of Aristotle's death: "That *Aristotle* drowned himself in *Euripus*, as despairing to resolve the cause of its reciprocation, or ebb and flow seven times a day, with this determination, *Si quidem ego non capio te, tu capies me*, was the assertion of *Procopius, Nazianzen, Justin Martyr*, and is generally believed among us" (7.13). The Latin phrase, meaning, "If I cannot comprehend you, you shall comprehend me," revolves around the Latin verb *capere*, which means to take in hand or seize, and shares its root with *captus*, prisoner. In its metaphorical sense, as here, the word means to comprehend or understand, but the visceral meaning of "capture" seems crucial: Aristotle, who represents the apex of human intellectual possibility for the culture in which this story circulated, drowns himself because he cannot capture the sea. Like King Canute's, Aristotle's authority stops at the water's edge.

But it's not only frustrated ambition that drives Aristotle, like Timon, to the surf. His desire to be contained in the sea – *tu capies me* – parallels the fundamentally religious insights that immersion generates. To be comprehended and made prisoner by a more-than-human oceanic world is Lear's problem, and Ferdinand's, and (perhaps most of all) Marina's. It's the shock that cures Maret's patients, and the instability that drives Othello mad. According to Plato, the purpose of philosophy was to explain away mysteries like the tides of Euripus; in the *Phaedo* (90c), Socrates cites these shifting tides as a metaphor for people who constantly change their opinions. In this philosophical model, as in Lucretius's, philosophy counteracts such intellectual waywardness; Socratic teaching generates stable truths. The lure of the sea, by contrast, promises different truths – experiential and coenaesthetic rather than intellectual – about humanity in the world. Bodies-in-water, drowning or swimming, experience the unstable and changing reality of nature.

Another name for stable truths about nature is science, and Thomas Browne's further remarks on the drowning of Aristotle make it clear that he rejects the legend because it contradicts early modern scientific thought. Browne notes that the tides should not have been too difficult for Aristotle to fathom: "And surely he that could sometimes sit down with high improbabilities, that could content himself, and think to satisfie others, that the variegation of Birds was from their living in the Sun, or erection made by deliberation of the Testicles, would not have been dejected unto death with this." Browne further cites a series of more recent authorities who testify that the Euripus flows four times daily, "according to the Law of the Sea." This Law, Browne argues, marks the separation between Aristotle's intellectual culture and his own: "Surely the Philosophy of flux and reflux was very imperfect of old among the Greeks and Latins; nor could they hold a sufficient theory thereof, who onely observed the Mediterranean, which in some places hath no ebb, and not much in any part." Being cut off from the Atlantic, with its more measurable tides, hampers Aristotle, but Browne's larger claim distinguishes early modern "Philosophy" or science. We moderns know how the world works, he says. And we are not likely to throw ourselves into the sea in frustration at its particulars. Browne recognizes that no human knowledge is absolute – in *Religio Medici* he argues that since Aristotle "understood the uncertainty of knowledge," he surely would not have drowned himself over the "flux and reflux of Euripus" – but he also treats his own limited knowledge as sufficient. Aristotle drowning represents, as Browne recognizes, a failure of the scientific mind. This image of failure underlies both the story's popularity and the hostility scientists have shown to it from Browne forward.

Moby-Dick

Browne's response to Aristotle emphasizes the contrast between two ways of thinking about the ocean: his own proto-scientific resistance to the legend, and the credulity of pre-scientific thinkers. This distinction recapitulates the familiar split between treating the ocean as a challenge to empirical understanding on the one hand, and seeing it as a divine Absolute, a God-space that humankind can see but not understand on the other. This dualism continues to define the cultural meanings of the sea long after Browne and Shakespeare. *Moby-Dick* maps precisely this difference onto its famous quasi-environmental chapter, "Does the Whale's Magnitude Diminish? – Will He Perish?" This chapter speaks about whales with two voices. Ishmael first lays out the historical and empirical evidence that whales seem to be decreasing in number and perhaps in size, and then insists that he, a dedicated believer in the symbolic importance of whales, will not accept these observable facts. First he's Thomas Browne, willing to face whatever he sees, and then a joyously demented Aristotle, hurling himself into mysterious waters. The evidence all points toward the whale's diminishment, from Pliny's (presumably unreliable) descriptions of eight-hundred-foot-long whales in classical antiquity to prodigious descriptions from more recent naturalists. The modern decrease in numbers is even easier for the whaleman to prove. "In former years," Ishmael notes, "these Leviathans, in small pods, were encountered oftener than at present, and, in consequence, the voyages were not so prolonged, and were also much more remunerative." Money and time tell him that whales are scarcer now. Even the withdrawal of certain species of whales from their former hunting grounds to remote Artic and Antarctic waters ("two firm fortresses," Ishmael calls them, "which, in all human probability, will for ever remain impregnable") cannot force him to admit that he and his fellow fishermen are destroying the species. He finds the appropriate land-based parallel when he compares the "humped herds of whales with the humped herds of buffalo," but he will not admit that whales, too, are in danger of "extermination."

The counterblast Ishmael provides to the empirical evidence of the whale's diminishment is theological: Leviathan, the beast who is God, cannot vanish. His attack on Pliny, which might have relied on skepticism about the classical author's maritime experience, instead takes place in the afterlife. "The whale of to-day is as big as his ancestors in Pliny's time," Ishmael says, "And if I ever go where Pliny is, I, a whaleman (more than he was), will make bold to tell him so." He argues that the whale-hunt is less efficient than the buffalo, but his central point emphasizes the symbolic potency of Leviathan. "Wherefore," he intones, "for all these things, we account the whale immortal in his species, however perishable in his individuality." Whales represent the eternal in Nature, and they quite explicitly exceed humanity's greatest accomplishments: "he once swam over the site of the Tuileries, and Windsor Castle, and the Kremlin." The "eternal whale" will survive the next Noah's flood, but as a symbol of resistance rather than control, "spout[ing] his frothed defiance to the skies." Melville himself may be less credulous than his narrator, and more willing to accept the empirical evidence of the decline of whale population, but Ishmael, enthralled by the whale's symbolic power, insists on the creature's eternity. To lose Leviathan, he insists, would mean losing everything: "the moot point is, whether Leviathan can long endure so wide a chase, and so remorseless a havoc; whether he must not at last be exterminated from the waters, and the last whale, like the last man, smoke his last pipe, and then himself evaporate in the final puff?" Apocalyptic discourses throve in Melville's ante-bellum America as in Stuart England and still in the twenty-first-century global village, but Ishmael's satiric tone suggests that an educated narrator like him does not fear fictions of "the last man." He will not go down like Aristotle, whether he can comprehend the sea or not. The dismal future at which Ishmael laughs, Timon of Athens embraces.

Timon

Timon's misanthropy expresses itself through his play's slowly build-ing oceanic topos. In the allegory of artistic making that opens the play, the poet describes his art as a ship on a strange sea:

> My free drift
> Halts not particularly, but moves itself
> In a wide sea of wax: no levell'd malice
> Infects one comma in the course I hold,
> But flies an eagle flight, bold, and forth on,
> Leaving no tract behind.

> (1.1.45–50)

The fantasy of power in this crux (successive editors have replaced "of wax" with "of verse," "of tax," and "awax") draws on the sense of wax as a moldable form, ready to accept poetic shaping. The mari-time imagery, from "drift" to "sea," further suggests that what the poet wants to control is the ocean. Timon's play measures human capacities against the sea as representation of an absolutely foreign nature. When the urban half of the play reaches its crisis in the mock-banquet, Timon presents his guests with bowls of water in lieu of a feast. Water here represents that which cannot be falsified, cannot mean anything other than what it means, and therefore cannot satisfy courtiers. "Smoke and lukewarm water / Is your perfection" (3.6.85–6). Timon snarls, after having claimed that his gift will transform aristocrats into animals: "Uncover, dogs, and lap" (3.6.82). Like Antony imagining Rome melting in the Tiber, Timon wants his city to vanish below the waves: "Sink, Athens! Henceforth hated be / Of Timon, man, and all humanity!" (3.6.100–1). The poet's fantasy "sea of wax" suggests a possible union of culture and nature, of shaping and being, but Timon's rage against built things rejects that hybrid order.

The play's abandonment of the city for woods and the "beached verge" in the final two acts, and Timon's servants recognition that they, like Lear and Poor Tom, have been abandoned in a stormy sea, continue the steady march toward the strand. Timon's monologues, like Pericles's storm-speeches, explicitly recall the central acts of *King Lear*. The Third Servant's shipwreck analogy parallels those scenes as well as the opening of *The Tempest*. "Leak'd is our bark," he laments, "And we, poor mates, stand on the dying deck, / Hearing the surges threat; we must all part / Into this sea of air" (4.2.19–22). The familiar metaphor of the ship of state being broken, part of Shakespeare's rhetoric since the *Henry VI* plays and of Western literature since *Antigone*, here broadens into a vision of an inhospitable "sea of air." The shift from the poet's form-receiving "sea of wax" to the third servant's community-sundering "sea of air" may, like comparable shifts in *Pericles*, map onto each play's two-author structure. But the common term in each metaphor ("sea") suggests that *Timon*, like *Pericles*, treats the sea as the world. When Timon's rejection of Athens reaches its apex, he sees the city as a ship in distress and diagnoses its problems as "the common wrack" (5.1.191). He stills loves his country, but will not help against Alcibiades's army because he has come to disdain "nature's fragile vessel" and "life's uncertain voyage" (5.1.200–1). For Timon, the world-sea is a place from which humanity needs to escape.

Timon rejects nature more emphatically than either Lear or Pericles because he understands the entire natural system as self-contradictory. Neither Edmund's "goddess" nor Pericles's "great vast," Timon's nature consumes itself, transforming an apparently orderly world into chaos. Even the world's divine principles impede themselves; Timon calls the sun and moon, "Twinn'd brothers of one womb, / Whose procreation, residence and birth / Scarce is dividant" (4.3.3–5). Nature here resembles Iago's self-negating nihilism. "Not nature," Timon says, "To whom all sores lay siege, can bear great fortune, / But by contempt of nature" (4.3.6–8). This natural world is a fully organized system that does not need divine control, but its destructive ecology leaves no place for man. In a term that Shakespeare probably borrows from Plutarch (or perhaps Lucian), Timon calls himself "*Misanthropos*" and says that he "hates mankind" (4.3.54), but it seems accurate to emphasize that he hates nature also. The first half of the play documents his rejection of the cultural world, but his attitude toward the natural environment is no less searing. Speaking to Alcibiades, Timon attributes his changeableness to the moon, but then suggests that the natural metaphor breaks down: "But then renew I could not like the moon; / There were no suns to borrow of" (4.3.69–70). Timon has become a dark moon orbiting a sunless planet, or a mariner without a shore: his world has no place for him.

In this context, his choice of the "hem of the sea" (5.4.66) for his final resting place locates him outside both social and natural ecologies. The sea-verge presents a boundary-space, full of instability and crisis. "[S]ick of this false world," he craves the beach for its violence: "Lie where the light foam of the sea may beat / Thy gravestone daily: make thine epitaph, / That death in me at others' lives may laugh" (4.3.378, 381–3). The mismatch between the "light foam" and its force to "beat" Timon's grave emphasizes how hard it is to conceptualize the sea's power; this unnatural nature is what Timon seeks but cannot, finally, enter. The marine verge promises an intimacy with natural violence and instability that even Timon cannot quite achieve. The "turbulent surge" that covers his body becomes his last perception of the world. Like Poor Tom, he sees waters rising.

In one of Shakespeare's most striking representations of ecological interdependence, Timon describes nature as a mutual ecology of theft:

> The sun's a thief, and with his great attraction
> Robs the vast sea; the moon's an arrant thief,
> And her pale fire she snatches from the sun;
> The sea's a thief, whose liquid surge resolves
> The moon into salt tears; the earth's a thief,
> That feeds and breeds by a composture stol'n
> From gen'ral excrement; each thing's a thief.
>   (4.3.439–45)

The struggle between sun, sea, moon, and earth defines the world-system, which produces new forms through "composture," or composting. The moon's "pale fire" – Nabokov, using the phrase for his novel of poetry and plagiarism, draws out this moment's crisis of linguistic meaning – reflects the sun's stolen energy, the sun steals moisture from the sea, and the sea "resolves" the moon. Unlike the pastoral harmony of *As You Like It* or Marvell's garden poems, the interrelated world here is a place of desperate struggle. It's also strikingly inhuman, lacking even the "universal wolf" of appetite that Ulysses sees in *Troilus and Cressida* (1.3.121). In this anonymous system of abstract forces, there is no room for personalities. Even the gods have been silenced.

Timon's multiple epitaphs presumably reveal authorial revision and textual corruption, but they also underline the play's anxiety about the relationship between language and nature. Timon's first epitaph, describing his "everlasting mansion" on the "beached verge of the salt flood," locates his corpse in its fixed-but-mobile symbolic place. But these lines cannot end his story. A soldier finds his tomb and reads his rejection of the human world: "Timon is dead, who hath outstretch'd his span: / Some beast read this; there does not live a man" (5.3.3–4). This inscription, presumably in English, serves as preamble to the two epitaphs that the soldier cannot read but only copy, presumably because they are in Latin. Alcibiades reads the two final epitaphs together, both of which appear in Plutarch. The first, which Plutarch attributes to Timon, rejects his own identity: "Here lies a wretched corse, of wretched soul bereft: / Seek not my name. A plague consume you, wicked caitiffs left!" (5.4.70–1). The second, which Plutarch attributes to Callimachus, embraces Timon's identity as the classic misanthropist: "Here lie I, Timon, who, alive, all living men did hate. / Pass by and curse thy fill, but pass and stay not here thy gait" (5.4.72–3). All four of these epitaphs emphasizes Timon's restlessness, his refusal of traditional forms like burial in the earth or the desire for a tomb to gather mourners together. The multiple epitaphs suggest that the hero pluralizes himself so that he cannot be reabsorbed into the cultural world. This last man remains outside of both culture and nature.

Shakespeare's play, if not his hero, acknowledges that the radical disjunction Timon craves is impossible. Alcibiades's final dozen lines, which follow the last two epitaphs, demonstrate how conventional social rhetoric attempts to reintegrate any exceptional figure. To the conquering general, even Timon's extreme rage cannot exclude him from the rebuilt social world. Alcibiades understands Timon's tomb to represent his return to a social and natural world that exists under the control of the classical gods. "[Y]et rich conceit," he says of Timon, "Taught thee to make vast Neptune weep for aye / On thy low grave, on faults forgiven" (5.4.77–9). To Alcibiades, the sea reveals Neptune's pathos, not the competitive ecology of theft. The general will make peace in Athens, and also tell "more" (5.4.81) of the story of the dead nobleman whose final wish is to be excluded from the tale of the city. "Let our drums strike" (5.4.85), intones Alcibiades in the play's last words. His proclamation insists that Timon's dreams of escape from nature and culture, his embrace of the sea and rejection of the land, cannot last. Any enduring civilization salvages what washes up on the beach.

Ahab

No one, not even Timon, rejects the world like Ahab. The captain goes down with the whale. His mad hunt for Moby-Dick through the Pacific, fueled by what Charles Olson calls "the will to overwhelm nature," finally leads him to the bottomless depths strapped to the whale's body. His last speech begins with an explicit rejection of the world in which humans live: "I turn my body from the sun." The loss of the *Pequod*, that "death-glorious ship," strands Ahab in his final grapple with the White Whale. All the world vanishes, and he is left, at last, diving toward the bottom with his hated adversary: "Sink all coffins and hearses to one common pool! and since neither can be mine, let me then tow to pieces, while still chasing thee, though tied to thee, thou damned whale! *Thus*, I give up the spear!" Choosing sea over land, death over life, whale over ship, Ahab drowns as he has lived. Defiant, melodramatic, alone, he represents a heroism too unconfined to rest in the social or natural worlds. Like Timon, Ahab, that "grand, ungodly, god-like man," rejects the spaces reserved for humankind. Both tragic figures may "have [their] humanities," as Captain Peleg says of Ahab, but neither rests comfortably in the world. The "great shroud of the sea" mantles both, Ahab in its depths and Timon on its shores. These figures' refusal to stay in the world seeks out the absolute alterity of the ocean. The last secret at the bottom is death.

Toward a Blue Cultural Studies

The true eye of the earth is water.
(*Gaston Bachelard*, Water and Dreams)

This World is Not Our Home

Look at the world through salty eyeballs, remembering that the fluid in our eyes tastes like the sea. Most of our world is water. Most of that water is salt. No matter what it looks like, what it makes us feel, how our bodies float on its swells, the ocean is no place to live. Like Timon, we make our mansions (when we make mansions) on the seashore, but they aren't built to last. Long ago we crawled out of the water. We can't go back.

Ecology Won't Keep Us Dry

Old tales of the God-sea and the climate of Enlightenment are fading, but our newer fables of ecological harmony can't keep us dry. The *oikos* of ecology too often gets imagined as a house built for people, a world fit for living in if not controlling. The sting of salt reminds us that the world isn't a happy story. Like Viola on the beach, humankind sits between fictions of Elysium and realities of Illyria. The productive consequences of ecological thinking – attention to the interdependence of different parts of nature, a decentering of human concerns, a deeper sense of continuities rather than distinctions – may help us salvage an increasingly inhospitable planet.

But hopes for a dry life, an easy, pastoral, sustainable relationship between nature and culture, seem as unlikely as a full season of calm seas. It's not that we don't want it. It's not that we shouldn't work toward it. It's that we won't get it.

The Ocean Rules the Weather

The driving force behind the climate, scientists tell us and poets remind us, is the ocean. This massive fluid reservoir holds the earth's heat and energy, and its circulation, from ocean currents to tropical storms to El Niño, powers our weather in a dynamic system we still cannot accurately model. From a certain point of view, the dominant actor in Anglo-American history for the past several thousand years has been the Gulf Stream, that torrid river in the sea whose northern tail heats the British Isles to a (fairly) comfortable temperature, and whose southern head steams out of the Caribbean and up the east coast of North America. The Gulf Stream's nutrient-rich waters fueled the massive biomass of the North Atlantic codfish grounds, which supported more than a millennium's worth of intensive fishing before being exhausted by factory trawlers in the late twentieth century. The current comprises a key part of the North Atlantic Gyre, the clockwise-rotating marine highway of prevailing winds and currents that crosses the Atlantic from Southwest Europe to the Caribbean basin, then turns northward into the Gulf of Mexico, flows out past Florida and up the coast of North America, and finally turns back eastwards across the North Atlantic. The early colonial expansion of Spain and Portugal, located near the jumping-off point for transatlantic travel, and the later growth of Great Britain and the Netherlands, located on the return route, arguably have been structured by the Gyre's peculiar geography. Living on land we sometimes forget the sea's dominance of our physical and cultural histories. We should remember.

Our Only Inexhaustible Resource is Language

It's not only the sea that's driving today's grim eco-thoughts. Bruno Latour suggests that we need a "politics of nature" to come to terms with global ecological crisis, and Timothy Morton thinks that we have to embrace a world without nature. But while literary criticism can't make fresh water out of salt or protect low-lying cities from tropical storms, it's through language and narrative that our culture has always grappled with living in an unstable, ocean-drenched environment. Shifting our focus from the supposed stability of land, with its pastoral and georgic master narratives, to a broader vision that embraces the maritime world and what Melville calls "this terraqueous globe" will mean abandoning certain happy fictions and replacing them with less comforting narratives. Fewer gardens, and more shipwrecks. But – and this is the key point – we have these narratives already. We just don't always put them at the center where they belong. The trick will be to replace the tragic, Promethean narrative of humanity's attempts to control nature – the story of Achilles fighting the river, as Michel Serres explains in *The Natural Contract* – with less epic, more improvisational stories of working-with an intermittently hostile world. We need sailors and swimmers to supplement our oversupply of warriors and emperors. We have these stories already: Odysseus swims to shore from his wrecked ship, Ishmael survives the wreck of the *Pequod*, Robinson Crusoe thrives in his island home. Marina, Egeon, Ferdinand, and Viola survive immersion, even if Othello and Timon do not. These are the stories we need. Stories we can use.

Shakespeare isn't Dead. He isn't Even Past.

When we look for the sea we see it. It's always there. Like the Cypriots in *Othello*, we may not understand the waters, but we know where to find them. The sea's overwhelming presence in our world gives us reasons to reread Shakespeare with salt in our eyes, to trace his oceanic symbolism from Egeon's solitary stoicism to the split negations of Viola and Iago. To think about how Poor Tom's fear of flood spills into the semi-opaque affirmations of Caliban and Marina. Because these stories – stories our culture stages for itself, year after year – can help unfold the rich and strange history of our imagined relationship with the biggest thing on our planet. Shakespeare's ocean is a shifting symbol whose meanings are never exhausted, emerging out of a geographic reality whose dynamic shapes early modern England was just coming to know. Its unreachable bottom conceals treasure and promises death. Shakespeare's sea stories uncover the vast range of things the ocean still means to our culture. Reading Shakespeare for the sea thus launches the vast and slightly quixotic project of a blue cultural studies, a way of looking at terrestrial literary culture from an offshore perspective, as if we could align ourselves with the watery element. It's true that we always need new stories, responsive to the radical changes underway in our natural environment. But Shakespeare's plays remind us that we also need to retell the old stories differently, to find in Edgar's imaginary cliffside and Marina's wayward journeys and Ariel's salt-infused music a painful and joyful history of coming to terms with a world of flux. A deep fascination with the ocean as the condition and boundary of our lives spills out of Shakespeare to his literary heirs. Alongside writers like Melville and Olson and Glissant, Shakespeare ask us to read for salt, to read as if certain narratives can help us embrace and endure ocean-driven disorder. Whether we can imitate Marina, or Queequeg, or even Poor Tom, isn't certain. But as the world grows bluer and less orderly, these are the stories we need.

Warm Water Epilogue

Writing this book, I swam every day in the salt water of Long Island Sound.

I cannot believe, despite Auden, that we know no ocean outside Romanticism.

The sea lures us, holds us, touches us. Our mother and our grave.

Cleopatra taught Mark Antony the secret way: "By sea, by sea" (3.7.40).

Reading the New Thalassology

This bibliographical essay outlines the new maritime humanities and then lists the works mentioned in this book. For a more traditional scholarly analysis, see my article, "Toward a Blue Cultural Studies: The Sea, Maritime Culture, and Early Modern English Literature," *Literature Compass* (forthcoming 2009).

The Med was Shakespeare's favorite ocean, and that's where the "new thalassology" was born. The term was coined in Nicholas Horden and Peregrin Purcell's *The Corrupting Sea: A Study of Mediterranean History* (Oxford: Blackwell, 2000). Recent responses include W. V. Harris's collection *Rethinking the Mediterranean* (Oxford: Oxford University Press, 2005); Edward Peters's "Quid nobis cum pelago?: The New Thalassology and the Economic History of Europe," *Journal of Interdisciplinary History* 34:1 (Summer 2003): 49–61; and Horden and Purcell's "The Mediterranean and 'the New Thalassology,'" *AHR* (June 2006): 722–40. New literary Mediterraneans appear in Tom Clayton, Susan Brock, and Vincente Forés's collection *Shakespeare and the Mediterranean* (Newark: University of Delaware Press, 2004), and Goran Stanivukovic's "Recent Studies of English Renaissance Literature of the Mediterranean," *English Literary Renaissance* 32 (2002): 168–83.

The maritime turn also aims more broadly. Following pioneering studies like Alain Corbin's *The Lure of the Sea: The Discovery of the Seaside in the Western World, 1750–1840* (Cambridge: Polity Press, 1994) and Barry Cunliffe's *Facing the Ocean: The Atlantic and Its Peoples, 8000 BC–AD 1500* (Oxford: Oxford University Press, 2001), historians are treating oceans and oceanic basins as organizing principles. Kären Wigen's *American History Review* forum, "Oceans of History" (June 2006), outlines the sub-field. Notable recent publications include W. Jeffrey Bolster's "Opportunities in Marine Environmental History," *Environmental History* 11 (2006): 1–31; Daniel Finamore's collection, *Maritime History as World History* (Gainesville: University of Florida Press, 2004); Greg Dening's *Mr. Bligh's Bad Language: Passion, Power, and Theatre on the Bounty* (Cambridge: Cambridge University Press, 1996); and *Beach Crossings: Voyaging Across Times, Cultures, And Self* (Philadelphia: University of Pennsylvania Press, 2004); Susan Rose's *The Medieval Sea* (London: Hambledon/ Continuum, 2007); Lisa Norling's *Captain Ahab Had a Wife: New England Women and the Whalefishery, 1720–1870* (Chapel Hill: University of North Carolina Press, 2000); Helen Rozwadowski's *Fathoming the Ocean: The Discovery and Exploration of the Deep Sea* (Cambridge: Belknap Press, 2005); and her collection, edited with David K. Van Keuren, *The Machine in Neptune's Garden: Historical Perspectives on Technology and the Marine Environment* (Sagamore Beach, MA: Science History Publication, 2006). Historical geographers have also turned to the sea; see David Lambert, Luciana Martins, and Miles Ogborn's "Currents, Visions and Voyages: Historical Geographies of the Sea," *Journal of Historical Geography* 32 (2006): 479–93.

The move "back to the sea" also relies on some suggestive theoretical works, including Gaston Bachelard's *Water and Dreams: An Essay on the Imagination of Matter*, Edith R. Farrell, trans. (Dallas: Dallas Institute of Humanities and Culture, 1983. [Orig. 1942]); Michel Foucault's "Of Other Spaces," Jay Miskowiec, trans., *Diacritics* 16 (1986): 22–27; and Luce Irigaray's "The 'Mechanics' of Fluids," in *This Sex Which is Not One*, Catherine Porter, trans. (Ithaca: Cornell University Press, 1985), 106–18. Recent theoretical works include two essays by Christopher Connery, "Ideologies of Land and Sea: Alfred Thayer Mahan, Carl Schmitt, and the Shaping of Global Myth Elements," *Boundary 2* 28:2 (2001): 173–201; and "There was No More Sea: The Suppression of the Ocean from the Bible to Hyperspace," *Journal of Historical Geography* 32 (2006): 494–511; Ivan Illich's, *H2O and the Waters of Forgetfulness: Reflections on the Historicity of "Stuff"* (Dallas: Dallas Institute of Humanities and

Culture, 1985); Philip Steinberg's *The Social Construction of the Ocean* (Cambridge: Cambridge University Press, 2001); and Jean-Didier Urbain's *At the Beach*, Catherine Porter, trans. (Minneapolis: University of Minnesota Press, 2003).

These historical and theoretical trends meet, as they often do, in literary studies. See, for example, Margaret Cohen's articles, "Fluid States: The Maritime in Modernity," *Cabinet* 16 (2004); and "Traveling Genres," *New Literary History* 34:3 (2003): 486; Joseph Roach's *Cities of the Dead: Circum-Atlantic Performance* (New York: Columbia University Press, 1996); Ian Baucom's *Specters of the Atlantic: Finance Capital, Slavery, and the Philosophy of History* (Durham: Duke University Press, 2005); and, in the early modern period, Bernhard Klein's two collections, *Fictions of the Sea: Critical Perspectives on the Ocean in British Literature and Culture* (Aldershot: Ashgate, 2002) and, coedited with Gesa Mackenthun, *Sea-Changes: Historicizing the Ocean* (London: Routledge, 2004). Shakespeareans might also enjoy Alexander Falconer's *Shakespeare and the Sea* (New York: Frederick Ungar, 1964); Philip Edwards's *Sea-Mark: The Metaphorical Voyage, Spenser to Milton* (Liverpool: Liverpool University Press, 1997); Michael Nerlich's *Ideology of Adventure: Studies in Modern Consciousness, 1100–1750*, Ruth Crowley, trans., Wlad Godzich, foreword (Minneapolis: University of Minnesota Press, 1987); Patricia Fumerton's *Unsettled: The Culture of Mobility and the Working Poor in Early Modern England* (Chicago: University of Chicago Press, 2006); John Gillis's *Islands of the Mind: How the Human Imagination Created the Atlantic World* (New York: Palgrave, 2004); Michael Witmore's *Culture of Accidents: Unexpected Knowledges in Early Modern England* (Stanford: Stanford University Press, 2001); and Peter Womack's "Shakespeare and the Sea of Stories," *Journal of Medieval and Early Modern Studies* 29:1 (Winter 1999): 169–87. For surveys of maritime literature, see Robert Foulke's *The Sea Voyage Narrative* (New York: Routledge, 2002); and Harold Francis Watson's *The Sailor in English Fiction and Drama, 1550–1800* (New York: Columbia University Press, 1931). I also recommend Lawrence Otto Goedde's *Tempest and*

Shipwreck in Dutch and Flemish Art: Convention, Rhetoric, and Interpretation (University Park: Penn State University Press, 1989).

These new trends respond in various ways to the massive surge of "Atlantic History." Many introductions to this thriving sub-field are available, including Alison Games's "Atlantic History: Definitions, Challenges, and Opportunities," *AHR* 111:3 (June 2006): 741–57; and her essay, "Beyond the Atlantic: English Globetrotters and Transoceanic Connections," *William and Mary Quarterly* 63:4 (October 2006): 675–97. Recent works in Atlantic history include David Armitage's *The Ideological Origins of the British Empire* (Cambridge: Cambridge University Press, 2000); and his collection, coedited with Michael J. Braddick, *The British Atlantic World, 1500–1800* (London: Palgrave, 2002); Bernard Bailyn's *Atlantic History: Concept and Countours* (Cambridge, MA: Harvard University Press, 2005); Paul Gilroy's *The Black Atlantic: Modernity and Double Consciousness* (Cambridge: Harvard University Press, 1993); and the works of Marcus Rediker, including *Between the Devil and the Deep Blue Sea: Merchant Seamen, Pirates and the Anglo-American Maritime World, 1700–1750* (Cambridge: Cambridge University Press, 1993); *Villains of All Nations: Atlantic Pirates in the Golden Age* (Boston: Beacon Press, 2005); and *The Slave Ship: A Human History* (New York: Viking, 2007). Recently Jack D. Greene, a major figure in Atlantic studies, has coedited with Philip Morgan, *Atlantic History: A Critical Appraisal* (Oxford: Oxford University Press, 2008). The field has also generated a series of response essays, including Peter A. Coclanis's "Atlantic World or Atlantic/World?" *William and Mary Quarterly* 63:4 (2006): 725–42; Lara Putnam's "To Study the Fragments/Whole: Microhistory and the Atlantic World," *Journal of Social History* 39:3 (2006): 615–30; and Paul Cohen's "Was There an Amerindian Atlantic?: Reflections on the Limits of a Historiographical Concept," *History of European Ideas* 34:4 (December 2008): 388–410.

The Atlantic was hardly the only new watery frontier for early modern Europe. The East also beckoned, inside and outside the Med, as shown in recent studies like Richmond Barbour's *Before*

Orientalism: London's Theater of the East, 1576–1626 (Cambridge: Cambridge University Press, 2003); Christopher Hodgkins's *Reforming Empire: Protestant Colonialism and Conscience in British Literature* (Columbia: University of Missouri Press, 2002); and Daniel Vitkus's *Turning Turk: English Theater and the Multicultural Mediterranean, 1570–1630* (New York: Palgrave, 2003). Recent studies of early modern maritime orientation include D. K. Smith's *The Cartographic Imagination in Early Modern England* (Aldershot: Ashgate, 2008); Tom Conley's *The Self-Made Map: Cartographic Writing in Early Modern France* (Minneapolis: University of Minnesota Press, 1996); several essays by Philip Edwards, including "Edward Hayes Explains Away Sir Humphrey Gilbert," *Renaissance Studies* 6:3–4 (1992): 270–86; and "Tragic Form and the Voyagers," in Jean-Pierre Maquerlot and Michéle Willems's *Travel and Drama in Shakespeare's Time* (Cambridge: Cambridge University Press, 1996), 75–86; Jonathan Bate's "Shakespeare's Islands," in *Shakespeare and the Mediterranean*, 289–307; T. J. Cribb's "Writing Up the Log: The Legacy of Hakluyt," in Steve Clark's *Travel Writing and Empire: Postcolonial Theory in Transit* (London: Zed Books, 1999), 100–12; Roger Kuin's "Querre-Muhau: Sir Philip Sidney and the New World," *Renaissance Quarterly* 51:2 (Summer 1998): 549–85; and James P. Helfers's "The Explorer or the Pilgrim?: Modern Critical Opinion and the Editorial Methods of Richard Hakluyt and Samuel Purchas," *Studies in Philology* 94:2 (1997): 160–86. Lloyd A. Brown's *The Story of Maps* (New York: Dover, 1979) remains a handy resource for cartographic history, alongside David Woodward's six-volume *History of Cartography* (Chicago: University of Chicago Press, 1987–98). Gunnar Olsson's *Abysmal: A Critique of Cartographic Reason* (Chicago: University of Chicago Press, 2007) provides theoretical perspective.

John Hattendorf's *The Boundless Deep: The European Conquest of the Oceans, 1450 to 1840* (Providence: John Carter Brown Library, 2003) provides an excellent illustrated introduction to transoceanic expansion. On European culture's transoceanic turn, I also recommend Eric Ash's *Power, Knowledge, and Expertise in Elizabethan England*

(Baltimore: Johns Hopkins University Press, 2004); Richard Grove's *Green Imperialism: Colonial Expansion, Tropic Island Edens, and the Origins of Environmentalism, 1600–1868* (Cambridge: Cambridge University Press, 1996), and (on a smaller scale), Elizabeth Mancke's "Early Modern Expansion and the Politicization of Oceanic Space," *Geographical Review* 89:2 (April 1999): 225–36. To supplement Anglophone histories, I recommend Josiah Blackmore's *Manifest Perdition: Shipwreck Narrative and the Disruption of Empire* (Minneapolis: University of Minnesota Press, 2002); Nicolás Wey-Gómez's *Tropics of Empire: Why Columbus Sailed South to the Indies* (Cambridge: MIT Press, 2008); and Jorge Cañizares-Esguerra's *Puritan Conquistadors: Iberianizing the Atlantic, 1550–1700* (Stanford: Stanford University Press, 2006), among others.

Turning to the ocean entails reconsidering the land-based tropes and narratives of environmentalism and ecology. Among early modern ecocritical works, I recommend Gabriel Egan's *Green Shakespeare: From Ecopolitics to Ecocriticism* (London: Routledge, 2006); Robert Watson's *Back to Nature: The Green and the Real in the Late Renaissance* (Philadelphia: University of Pennsylvania Press, 2006); and Ken Hiltner's *Milton and Ecology* (Cambridge: Cambridge University Press, 2003). In a theoretical context, I have benefited from Pierre Hadot's *The Veil of Isis: An Essay on the History of the Idea of Nature*, Michael Chase, trans. (Cambridge: Harvard University Press, 2006); Bruno Latour's *Politics of Nature: How to Bring the Sciences into Democracy*, Catherine Porter, trans. (Cambridge: Harvard University Press, 2004); Timothy Morton's *Ecology Without Nature* (Cambridge, MA: Harvard University Press, 2007); and Val Plumwood's *Environmental Culture: The Ecological Crisis of Reason* (London: Routledge, 2002). For a depressing but enlightening view of today's oceans, see Richard Ellis, *The Empty Ocean* (Washington: Island Press, 2004).

I quote Shakespeare throughout from the Arden editions, published in London by Thomson Learning: *The Tempest* (Virginia Mason Vaughan and Alden Vaughan, eds, 1999); *Pericles* (Suzanne Gosset, ed., 2004); *Othello* (E. A. J. Honingmann, ed., 1997); *King Richard III*

(Anthony Hammond, ed., 1981); *King Lear* (R. A. Foakes, ed., 1997); *The Comedy of Errors* (R. A. Foakes, ed., 1962); *Macbeth* (Kenneth Muir, ed., 1962); *Julius Caesar* (David Daniell, ed., 1998); *King Henry VIII* (Gordan McMullan, ed., 2001); *Twelfth Night* (Keil Elam, ed., 2008); *Hamlet* (Ann Thompson and Neil Taylor, eds, 2006); *King Henry IV Part 1* (David Scott Kastan, ed., 2002); *Antony and Cleopatra* (John Wilders, ed., 1995); *Timon of Athens* (H. J. Oliver, ed., 1959); *Troilus and Cressida* (David Bevington, ed., 1998).

My preface opens with an echo of "The Seafarer," in *The Earliest English Poems*, Michael Alexander, ed. (New York: Penguin, 1991). I also refer to Édouard Glissant's *Poetics of Relation*, Betsy Wing, trans. (Ann Arbor: University of Michigan Press, 1997); and Pierre Hadot's *Veil of Isis*. I quote Derek Walcott's "The Sea is History" from *Selected Poems*, Edward Baugh, ed. (New York: Farrar, Straus, and Giroux, 2007), 137; and Marvel's "Upon Appleton House" from *The Complete Poems*, Elizabeth Story Donno, ed. (New York: Penguin, 1985). My first epigraph is from "Childe Harold's Pilgrimage" (4:49), in *Byron's Poetry*, Frank D. McConnel, ed. (New York: Norton, 1978).

The opening of Chapter 1 responds to Ian Baucom's "Hydrographies," *Geographical Review* 89:2 (1999): 301–13. I quote Glissant's "Ocean" from *The Collected Poems of Édouard Glissant*, Jeff Humphries and Melissa Manolas, trans. (Minneapolis: University of Minnesota Press, 2005); and *Moby-Dick* from Hershal Parker and Harrison Haywood's second Norton edition (New York: Norton, 2002). My understanding of the early modern ocean as a space of risk, disorientation, and chance derives from Ulrich Kinzel's "Orientation as a Paradigm in Maritime Modernity," in Klein's *Fictions of the Sea*. I won't summarize the massive bibliographies of *The Tempest* and *King Lear* (or any other Shakespeare plays), but I did find several sources especially helpful, including David Bergeron's "The Tempest/*The Tempest*," *Essays in Literature* 7 (1980): 3–9; Ralph Berry's "Metamorphoses of the Stage," *Shakespeare Quarterly* 33:1 (1982): 5–16; Peter Hulme and William Sherman's collection *"The Tempest" and Its Travels* (Philadelphia: University of Pennsylvania Press, 2000); B. J. Sokal's

A Brave New World of Knowledge: Shakespeare's The Tempest *and Early Modern Epistemology* (Madison: Farleigh Dickinson University Press, 2003); and, though it shows its age, G. Wilson Knight's *The Shakespearean Tempest* (London: Methuen, 1932). This chapter refers to T. S. Eliot's *The Waste Land,* in *The Complete Poems and Plays, 1909–1950* (New York: Harcourt Brace Jovanovich, 1971); Rachel Carson's *The Sea Around Us* (Oxford: Oxford University Press, 1951); Plato's *Laws,* Trevor J. Saunders, ed. (New York: Penguin, 2005); the King James *Bible*, David Norton, ed. (New York: Penguin, 2006); Robert Norman's *The Safeguard of Sailors* (London, 1584); Joseph Conrad's *The Mirror of the Sea* (Marlboro, VT: Marlboro Press, 1988); Isaac Vossius's *Treatise Concerning the Motion of the Seas and Winds* (London, 1677); Geoffrey Chaucer's "The Man of Law's Tale," *The Riverside Chaucer,* third ed., F. N. Robinson, ed. (Boston: Houghton Mifflin, 1987); W. H. Auden's *The Sea and the Mirror: A Commentary on Shakespeare's* The Tempest, Arthur Kirsch, ed. (Princeton: Princeton University Press, 2003); Victor Hugo's *Toilers of the Sea,* James Hogarth, trans. (New York: Modern Library, 2002); and A. F. Falconer's *Shakespeare and the Sea.*

In Chapter 2, I engage Hans Blumenberg's reading of Lucretius, *Shipwreck with Spectator: Paradigm of a Metaphor for Existence*, Steven Rendall, trans. (Cambridge: MIT Press, 1997). I quote Lucretius from the Loeb edition, W. H. D. Rouse, trans., Martin F. Smith, rev. (Cambridge: Harvard University Press, 1992); and Charles Olson from *The Maximus Poems*, George F. Butterick, ed. (Berkeley: University of California Press, 1983); and *Call Me Ishmael: A Study of Melville* (San Francisco: City Light Books, 1947). On the classical resonance of the storm in *Othello*, I rely on Teoman Sipahigil's "Ovid and the Tempest in *Othello*," *Shakespeare Quarterly* 44:4 (Winter 1993): 468–71.

The first interlude, "Sunken Treasure," mashes together Father Mapple's sermon and the "Brit" chapter in *Moby-Dick* with Clarence's dream in *Richard III*.

Chapter 3 draws on Nicholas Orme's *Early British Swimming, 55 BC–AD 1719* (Exeter: Short Run Press, 1983); and Michael West's "Spenser, Everard Digby, and the Renaissance Art of Swimming," *Renaissance Quarterly* 26:1 (Spring 1973): 11–22. The chapter refers to Frost's lyric, "Neither out far nor in deep," in *The Poetry of Robert Frost*, Edward Connery Lathem, ed. (New York: Henry Holt, 1969); Yann Martel's *Life of Pi* (New York: Harcourt, 2001); Günter Grass's *Crabwalk,* Krishna Winston, trans. (New York: Harcourt, 2002); Edmund Pet's *Lamentable News* (London, 1607); John King's *Lectures on Jonah* (London, 1594); Thomas Jackson's *The Raging Tempest Stilled* (London, 1623); Augustine's *De Beata Vita, The Works of Saint Augustine* (Hyde Park: New City Press, 1990); William Gilbert's *De magente* (London, 1600); William Bourne's *Regiment for the Sea* (London, 1580); Laurence Goedde's *Tempest and Shipwreck in Dutch and Flemish Art*; Alain Corbin's *The Lure of the Sea*; and Olson's *Call Me Ishmael.* I also recommend several recent works on swimming, including Akiko Busch's *Nine Ways to Cross a River: Midstream Reflections on Swimming and Getting There from Here* (New York: Bloomsbury, 2007); Robert Lawrence France's *Deep Immersion: The Experience of Water* (Sheffield, CT: Green Frigate Books, 2003); Lynne Cox's *Swimming to Antarctica: Tales of a Long-Distance Swimmer* (New York: Harvest, 2005); and (most entertaining of all) Charles Sprawson's *Haunts of the Black Masseur: The Swimmer as Hero* (Minneapolis: University of Minnesota Press, 2000).

In Chapter 4, I quote Brathwaite's poetry from *The Arrivants: A New World Trilogy* (Oxford: Oxford University Press, 1973), and Walcott's from *Selected Poems.* The excerpt from Dr. Maret comes from Corbin's *Lure of the Sea.* I refer to Euripides's *Iphigenia at Tauris* (Philadelphia: University of Pennsylvania Press, 1999); elliptically to Mrs. Bennett's love of sea-bathing in Jane Austen's *Pride and Prejudice* (New York: Penguin, 2002); to W. H. Auden's *The Enchafèd Flood, or the Romantic Iconography of the Sea* (London: Faber and Faber, 1951); James Joyce's *Ulysses* (New York: Vintage, 1986); John Flavell's

Navigation Spiritualiz'd (London, 1698); Michel Serres's *The Natural Contract*, Elizabeth MacArthur and William Paulson, trans. (Ann Arbor: University of Michigan Press, 1995); *Edmund Spenser's Poetry*, second ed., Hugh Maclean, ed. (New York: Norton, 1982); Margaret Cavendish's "The Sea-Goddess," in *The Oxford Book of the Sea*, Jonathan Raban, ed. (Oxford: Oxford University Press, 1992), 78–9; Jean-Didier Urbain's *At the Beach*; Longinus's *Of the Sublime* (New York: Hackett, 1991); Edmund Burke's *A Philosophical Enquiry into the Origins of Our Ideas of the Sublime and Beautiful*, Adam Philips, ed. (Oxford: Oxford University Press, 2009); Immanuel Kant's *Observations on the Feeling of the Beautiful and Sublime*, John Goldthwait, trans. (Berkeley: University of California Press, 2004); and *Addison's Essays from the Spectator* (Adamant Media, 2001).

My interlude on piracy conjures up a vast bibliography, starting with the seminal work of Marcus Rediker. I also recommend Barbara Fuchs's "Faithless Empires: Pirates, Renegadoes, and the English Nation," *ELH* 67 (2000): 45–69; Claire Jowitt's "'Et in Arcadia Ego': The Politics of Pirates in the *Old Arcadia, New Arcadia*, and *Urania*," *Early Modern Literary Studies* 16 (October 2007): 5.1–36; Jacques Lezra's *Unspeakable Subjects: The Genealogy of the Event in Early Modern Europe* (Stanford: Stanford University Press, 1997); and Simon Palfrey's "The Rape of Marina," *Shakespearean International Yearbook* 7 (2007): 140–54. For mind-expanding if slightly dated fun, I also suggest Peter Lamborn Wilson's work of outlaw scholarship, *Pirate Utopias: Moorish Corsairs and European Renegadoes* (New York: Autonomedia, 2003), and Wilson's anarchist writings, written under the pen name Hakim Bey, *TAZ: The Temporary Autonomous Zone* (New York: Autonomedia, 2003).

In considering the relationship between Shakespeare and Homer in Chapter 5, I drew on a series of recent articles, including Sarah Dewar-Watson's "Shakespeare's Dramatic Odysseys: Homer as a Tragicomic Model in *Pericles* and *The Tempest*," *Classical and Modern Literature* 25/1 (2005): 23–40; Sara Hanna's "Shakespeare's Greek World: The Temptations of the Sea," in *Playing the Globe: Genre and*

Geography in English Renaissance Drama, John Gillies and Virginia Mason Vaughan, eds (Madison: Farleigh Dickinson University Press, 1998), 107–28; and Yves Peyré's "Shakespeare's *Odyssey*," in *Shakespeare and the Mediterranean*, 230–42. On Spanish and Portuguese disputes in the Pacific, see Jerry Brotton, *Trading Territories: Mapping the Early Modern World* (London: Reaktion, 2003). The chapter refers to Hugo Grotius's *Mare Liberum* (1609); John Seldon's *Mare Clausum* (London, 1635); Phineas Fletcher's *Piscatorie Eclogues* (London, 1633); William Diaper's *Nereides, or Sea-Eclogues* (London, 1712); Edward Hayes's account of Sir Humphrey Gilbert, in Hakluyt's *Principal Navigations*, 14 vols. (New York: AMS Press, 1965); Luiz vaz de Camões's *Lusiads*, Landeg White, trans. (Oxford: Oxford University Press, 2002); Ezra Pound's *The Cantos* (New York: New Directions, 1996); Northrop Frye, *The Secular Scripture* (Cambridge: Harvard University Press, 1976); and Philip Sidney, *The Countess of Pembroke's Arcadia*, Maurice Evans, ed. (New York: Penguin, 1987).

Chapter 6 quotes Thomas Browne, *Vulgar Errors* (London, 1672); Plato, *Phaedo* (New York: Gramercy Books, 1942); and Thomas Browne's *Religio Medici* (Oxford: Clarendon Press, 1972). The chapter also refers to Sprawson's *Haunts of the Black Masseur: The Swimmer as Hero*; Vladimir Nabokov's *Pale Fire* (New York: Everyman's Library, 1992); and Olson's *Call Me Ishmael*.

My conclusion quotes Gaston Bachelard's *Water and Dreams* and discusses Bruno Latour's *Politics of Nature* and Timothy Morton's *Ecology without Nature*.

My epilogue responds in part to Auden's *The Enchaféd Flood, or the Romantic Iconography of the Sea*.

For readers (like me) who enjoy a good salty tale but have read through the usual suspects (Conrad, Melville, Stevenson, Cooper, O'Brian), I recommend Jane Austen's *Sanditon*, Margaret Drabble, ed.(New York: Penguin, 1974); C. R. Boxer's translation, updated by Josiah Blackmore, *The Tragic History of the Sea* (Minneapolis: University of Minnesota Press, 2001); Fred D'Aguiar's *Feeding the Ghosts* (New York: Harper Collins, 2000); Daniel Defoe's *The Storm*,

Richard Hamblyn, ed. (New York: Penguin, 2005); John Fowles's *Shipwreck* (Boston: Little, Brown, 1975); Saint-John Perse's *Selected Poems*, Mary Ann Caws, ed. (New York: New Directions, 1982); and Iris Murdoch's *The Sea, the Sea* (London: Chatto and Windus, 1978).

Further reading can be found in a handful of bibliographies and anthologies, including Robert Baldwin's "A Bibliography of the Sea, Shipwreck, and Water in Western Literature and Art," *Bulletin of Bibliography* 48:3 (1991): 153–70; Keith Huntress's *Narratives of Shipwrecks and Disasters, 1586–1860* (Ames: Iowa State University Press, 1974); Peter Jay's poetry anthology *The Sea! The Sea!* (London: Anvil Press/Continuum, 2006); a special issue of the poetry journal *Agenda*, entitled *Poems on Water* (2006); Jonathan Raban's *The Oxford Book of the Sea* (Oxford: Oxford University Press, 2002); and Donald Wharton's compilation *In the Trough of the Sea: Selected American Sea-Deliverance Narratives, 1610–1766* (Westport: Greenwood, 1979).

Index